PEOPLE TO REMEMBER

30 Stories and Activities About Saints and Heroes for Youth Today

Janaan Manternach
and
Carl J. Pfeifer

PAULIST PRESS
New York/Mahwah

The stories contained in this book were previously published in *Faith Today* by National Catholic News Service.

Cover and interior art and design by Gloria Claudia Ortíz

Library of Congress Cataloguing in Publication Data

Manternach, Janaan.
    People to remember.

    Summary: Presents brief biographies of thirty saints and humanitarians including Pope John XXIII, Louis Braille, St. Frances of Rome, and Joan of Arc. Each selection is followed by review questions, a puzzle, poem, and prayer.
    1. Christian saints—Biography—Juvenile literature.
2. Christian biography—Juvenile literature. 3. Youth—Prayer-books and devotions—English. [1. Saints. 2. Christian biography. 3. Catholic Church—Prayer books and devotions. 4. Prayer books and devotions].
I. Pfeifer, Carl J. II. Title.

BX4658.M413 1987   ~~270~~   [920]   87-6992
ISBN 0-8091-6568-6 (pbk.)

Published by Paulist Press
997 Macarthur Boulevard
Mahwah, New Jersey 07430

Printed and bound in the
United States of America

Contents

ST. FRANCES OF ROME:
A Noble Family
1384-1440

Frances grew up in a wealthy, noble family in Rome. She was raised in luxury.

While she was still a young girl, her parents arranged for her to marry a young nobleman named Lorenzo. Lorenzo and his family loved Frances. Lorenzo's sister, Vanozza, became her best friend.

She resolved to serve God by being a good wife and mother. She treated the servants more like brothers and sisters. What time she had to herself she spent in prayer and in going about the city helping poor people. The rich people of Rome made fun of Frances for her concern about the poor.

Lorenzo and Frances had three children. Frances raised the children and taught them. Her rich relatives could not understand why she did that. They all hired nurses to care for their children, and tutors to teach them.

Once when the Tiber River flooded Rome, many poor people were hungry, homeless and sick. Frances was so generous that her father-in-law was upset. She was giving away food, clothes, and family possessions. For a while he took all house keys from her.

He soon changed his mind about his daughter-in-law. "You have found the secret of real happiness," he told Frances one day. "It is love, love that grows the more you give it away."

Lorenzo, too, encouraged Frances in her compassion for the poor of the city. She sold her jewels and expensive clothes to have more money to share with those in need.

Then a war arose. Farms around Rome were burned. Houses in the city were destroyed. Hundreds of people were homeless. Lorenzo was taken captive. So was one of her sons. Their palace was partially destroyed. Frances, her other children and Vanozza lived in a corner of the palace. Her second son died there.

The Tiber flooded again. Frances and Vanozza went all over Rome begging medicines, bandages, and food for the sick. They set up a soup kitchen for the hungry and begged food for them.

Finally the war ended. Lorenzo was able to come back. But he was not well. Frances was delighted to have her husband back with her. They loved each other very much. She cared for him and he allowed her freedom to follow a dream she had had since she was a child. She had always wanted to start a congregation of women to serve the poor and needy.

Now Frances was able to organize a group of women to work with the poor. They lived at home with their families but gave all their free time to works of charity. Later some of the unmarried women decided to live together in community.

A great sadness came to Frances when Lorenzo died. They had known and loved one another most of their lives. They were married forty years.

Frances missed Lorenzo very much. She spent more time in prayer and helping the poor. She decided to live in community with the other women she had brought together.

When Frances died, the people of Rome believed she was a saint. St. Frances is patroness of Rome. Her feastday is March 9.

ST. FRANCES OF ROME

Using the clues below,
work the crossword puzzle.

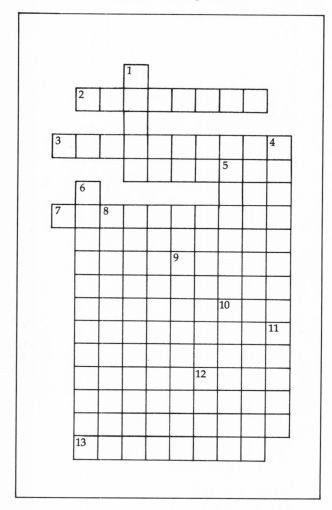

DOWN
1. A river in Rome
4. The woman the story is about
5. What the people thought she was when she died
6. Another name for a group of people
8. This is what she is to Rome
9. The opposite of men
10. Frances' best friend
11. Something that her husband gave her the freedom to follow

ACROSS
2. In Frances and Lorenzo's family there were three of these
3. Frances' husband
7. What Frances had for the poor
12. City where Frances grew up
13. Frances' husband's title

TO PRAY AND REMEMBER

All-powerful Father,
God of goodness,
you provide for all your creation.
Give us an effective love for our brothers and sisters
who suffer from lack of food.
Help us do all we can to relieve their hunger,
that they may serve you with carefree hearts.

(NEW SAINT JOSEPH PEOPLE'S PRAYER BOOK edited by Rev. Evans, Catholic Book Publishing Co. New York, 1980, prayer #330, pp. 255-256)

TO THINK AND TALK ABOUT

1. How did the rich people of Rome feel about Frances' concern for the poor?
2. What caused Frances' father-in-law to change his mind about her?
3. How did Frances realize her dream?

TO READ AND ENJOY:

A Storybook:

STONE SOUP by Marcia Brown (Charles Scribner's Sons, 597 Fifth Ave., New York, N. Y. 10017, 1947)

A Poem:

FRANCES OF ROME

Where the poor were
Frances was there
To clothe and to feed
To heal and to care.

Where the poor were
Her women went
Praying and helping
Their lives were spent.

(Tiber, Children, Lorenzo, Frances, Saint, Congregation, Compassion, Patroness, Women, Vanozza, Dream, Rome, Nobleman)

POPE JOHN XXIII:
Changing With the Times
1881-1963

Angelo grew up in a small village in Italy. His parents rented a small farm. They grew grapes and vegetables. They were proud to be farmers.

Angelo's father, John, loved to work in the fields. He dreamed of the day when he would be able to own his own vineyard. He hoped that his children would love farming as much as he did.

Angelo was the oldest son. He had twelve brothers and sisters. His father counted most on him to grow up to help him on the farm.

But Angelo didn't like farming. He felt bad that he did not enjoy working on the farm as his father did. His family had always been farmers. Everyone he knew seemed happy on the farms.

It wasn't that Angelo hated hard work. He liked another kind of work. He liked to study and to learn.

His father and mother were proud of Angelo's work in the small village school. They encouraged him to learn, but they wanted him to work on the farm with them as well.

Soon Angelo knew everything that he could learn in the village school. His parents let him go to a bigger school in a town about five miles away. Angelo walked to and from school. He did chores on the farm, too.

The priest in his village was a friend of Angelo's father and mother. Fr. Rebuzzini helped Angelo with his lessons.

But his parents kept wishing their son would be like the rest of the family. They hoped he would still become a farmer. But they knew in their hearts that Angelo wanted to be a priest rather than a farmer.

Fr. Rebuzzini encouraged Angelo. The good priest talked with Angelo's mother and father. He told them he thought God was calling their son to be a priest. So finally Angelo's parents let their boy go off to the city to study to become a priest.

It was a hard change for them. It was hard, too, for Angelo. He loved the new studies, but he missed his family. He slowly learned to deal with the changes he was experiencing.

Eventually Angelo Roncalli became a priest. He lived through many changes. He worked with the poor. He served in the army. He taught in the seminary. He wrote books. He was a diplomat. He lived in many parts of the world. He became a bishop. He became a cardinal.

Then as an old man he was chosen to be Pope. He took his father's name, calling himself Pope John XXIII. Those who elected him hoped that he would keep everything the way it was in the Church. They knew he was old. They felt he would not change anything.

But Pope John XXIII knew change was needed. He learned as a child on his parents' farm how hard but how important it can be to change. As Pope John, Roncalli started more changes in the Church than had happened in hundreds of years.

POPE JOHN XXIII

Find the 14 words hidden in the puzzle. They may be
vertical, horizontal or diagonal. All the words are in the story.

R	O	N	C	A	L	L	I	Z	L
X	C	S	I	P	O	P	E	A	E
P	H	C	T	J	O	H	N	N	A
R	A	H	A	U	V	I	W	G	R
I	N	O	L	Q	D	V	O	E	N
E	G	O	Y	R	J	Y	K	L	M
S	E	L	A	F	G	X	G	O	D
T	S	C	B	I	S	H	O	P	Z
L	R	E	B	U	Z	Z	I	N	I

TO PRAY AND REMEMBER

Heavenly Father,
you have created us in such a way
that each has some state in life to pursue
for the good of the whole human race
and your holy Church.
Help me to know my vocation
and to follow it with joy and dedication.
No matter what problem I may encounter,
let me never lose hope,
aware that you have given me the talents
to succeed in any state to which you call me.

(New St. Joseph's People's Prayer Book, prayer #1252, p. 936)

TO THINK AND TALK ABOUT

1. What was Angelo's favorite kind of work?
2. Why was Angelo's desire to become a priest hard on his parents?
3. What was the most important thing that Angelo, as Pope John XXIII, did for the Catholic Church?

TO READ AND ENJOY:

A Storybook:

HOPE FOR THE FLOWERS by Trina Paulus (Paulist Press, 997 Macarthur Boulevard, Mahwah, New Jersey 07430, 1972)

A Poem:

POPE JOHN XXIII

Farm boy
Angelo.
Went to school,
studied hard.
Became a priest,
bishop, cardinal,
Pope.
Brought about
changes and
gave our Church
hope.

(Angelo, Italy, John, study, learn, school priest, Rebuzzini, God, bishop, cardinal, pope, Roncalli, changes)

5

DOROTHY DAY:
Saint of the Slums
1897-1980

Dorothy Day was about eight when her family moved from California to Chicago. She grew up in Chicago.

Her father worked for a newspaper. So did her brother, Donald. They were both good writers. Dorothy's mother cared for the family.

Already as a child Dorothy loved books. She read for hours. She had good friends, and enjoyed playing. But books had a special place in her home.

One day when Dorothy was about fourteen, Donald urged Dorothy to visit Chicago's West Side. He said it was very different from the neighborhood where they lived.

A few days later Dorothy walked around the West Side. The houses looked so old and poor. The people who lived in them were poor. Dorothy was sad to see how much they suffered. She was just a teenager, but she felt that God wanted her somehow to help poor working people.

After high school she went to the University of Illinois. She studied hard. She spent many nights reading. She was learning ideas about why people are poor. She read books about how to help people.

The more she learned the less her faith in God seemed to matter. She no longer felt Jesus Christ was important to her. She also became restless. She wanted to do something more than study.

She went to New York and became a newspaper reporter. She saw first-hand how people suffered because they could not get jobs. She was arrested and put in prison for taking the side of the workers. She worked as a volunteer in a hospital ward for poor people.

She wanted to do more but did not know what to do. She began to pray again. She became a Catholic. One evening Dorothy knelt in the National Shrine of the Immaculate Conception in Washington, D.C. She begged God to show her how best to use her talents to help the poor.

When she got back home to New York, she found a man waiting to see her. His name was Peter Maurin. He and Dorothy talked and talked. Peter suggested that Dorothy start a newspaper for workers. She liked the idea. She called the newspaper, *The Catholic Worker*. It cost a penny. It still does.

Dorothy and Peter then opened a "house of hospitality" for the poor. Poor people could come there for free food, clothes, and a place to sleep. Dorothy lived right there. Her door was always open to anyone who had a problem or just wanted to talk.

For the rest of her life Dorothy Day lived with the poor. She continued writing her newspaper for working men and women. She and Peter opened houses of hospitality in other cities. She traveled all over the country to share her ideas about helping the poor. She took part in many strikes and protests. She suffered much because of her ideas. No matter how busy she was, she prayed and read the Bible an hour or two each day.

Many people believe Dorothy Day was a saint.

DOROTHY DAY

Unscramble the words below. All the words are in the story.

HTCOACIL

GOCIHAC

SPNAEPWER

OHTRODY

EILBB

NMURAIU

YTSPOHTLAII

KWREOR

NLLOIISI

SSTRPOTE

TO PRAY AND REMEMBER

PSALM 121

I lift up my eyes toward the mountains;
  whence shall help come to me?
My help is from the Lord,
  who made heaven and earth.
May he not suffer your foot to slip;
  may he slumber not who guards you:
Indeed he neither slumbers nor sleeps,
  the guardian of Israel.
The Lord is your guardian; the Lord is your shade;
  he is beside you at your right hand.
The sun shall not harm you by day,
  nor the moon by night.
The Lord will guard you from all evil;
  he will guard your life.
The Lord will guard your coming and your going,
  both now and forever.

(New American Bible)

TO THINK AND TALK ABOUT

1. What is one thing that Dorothy Day, as a teen-ager, learned about herself?

2. What are some things that Dorothy Day did to help the poor?
3. What special thing did Dorothy Day do every day, no matter how busy she was?

TO READ AND ENJOY:

A Storybook:

HARLEQUIN AND THE GIFT OF MANY COL-ORS by Remy Charlip (Parents' Magazine Press, 52 Vanderbilt Ave., New York, N.Y. 10017, 1973)

A Poem:

DOROTHY DAY

She fed the poor in winter
And invited them inside.
Her door was always open
For people who had cried.
She prayed and read the Bible
For an hour every day.
She was a caring woman.
Her name is Dorothy Day.

(Catholic, Chicago, newspaper, Dorothy, Bible, Maurin, hospi-tality, worker, Illinois, protests)

PAULO FREIRE:
Helping Adults Learn
1921-

Paulo was just eleven. He was hungry. It had been months since he had eaten a decent meal. His empty stomach hurt so much he could not do well in school.

Everyone around him was as poor as he was. But he remembered the nice home his family had when he was younger. His parents lost everything in the depression. Now Paulo was as poor as everyone else in the slums of Recife, Brazil.

"When I grow up," he thought one day, "I'm going to do something so children won't have to be hungry and poor the way we are now." Paulo promised God that he would study and work hard to find a way to help the poor improve their lives.

He was lucky to be able to continue going to school. He studied hard, never forgetting the millions of people who were poor and hungry. "What is the key to helping them make their lives better?" he kept asking himself. "How can I help break the cycle of poverty that keeps people down?"

At the university he discovered an answer. "Most of the poor men and women in Recife cannot read or write. They have no education. If I can find a way to help them learn to read, they will feel better about themselves. They will also discover why they and so many millions are so poor."

So Paulo Freire created a new approach to helping poor men and women learn to read. He believed that even the poorest, most uneducated man or woman had the ability to think. Instead of telling them what he thought they needed to know, he decided to draw out of them the things they never knew they knew.

He went out into the poorest sections of Recife to test his new methods on the poorest of the poor. He showed them photographs of places like those in which they lived. He encouraged them to talk about the pictures. He listened. He helped them discover what the words they spoke looked like when written. Gradually they learned to read.

But more important to Paulo, these poor men and women now had a new feeling about themselves. "Before this, words meant nothing to me; now they speak to me and I can make them speak," one woman said with tears of pride and joy.

"I now realize I am a man, an educated man," said an older man with a smile.

"We were blind," a young woman added enthusiastically; "now our eyes have been opened."

These poor men and women were also discovering why they were all so poor even when they worked hard. They could now see that they were kept poor by systems that made others rich. They began to realize that they could work to change that unjust situation.

Some of the powerful and rich leaders in Brazil did not like what the poor were learning. They forced Paulo Freire to leave his homeland. But they could not stop him from helping poor people in other countries learn to read and to discover how to make their lives better. They could never make him forget the promise he made to God when he was eleven years old and poor.

PAULO FREIRE

Using the clues below, work the crossword puzzle.

```
 1 [ ][ ][ ][ ][ ][ ]
                    2 [ ]
 3 [ ][ ][ ][ ]       [ ]
 4 [ ]  5 [ ]         [ ]       6 [ ]
 [ ]    [ ]  7 [ ][ ][ ][ ][ ][ ][ ][ ]
 8 [ ][ ][ ][ ]        [ ]
 [ ]    [ ]  9 [ ][ ][ ][ ][ ]
 [ ]    [ ]            [ ]
 [ ]
```

DOWN
1. Paulo Freire knew what it was like to be_____.
2. Paulo helped people in his hometown to_____and to write.
4. Paulo's parents lost everything in the_____.
5. Paulo knew that people were kept poor by_____ that made others rich.
6. Paulo Freire's homeland is_____.
7. Paulo did things so that people wouldn't be_____ and poor.

ACROSS
1. When Paulo Freire was young he made a_____ to God.
3. Paulo grew up in_____Brazil.
7. Paulo was forced to leave his_____.
8. Paulo was only_____when he promised God he would do something about the poor.
9. Paulo's family name is_____.

TO PRAY AND REMEMBER

Lord,
may everything we do
begin with your inspiration,
continue with your help,
and reach perfection under your guidance.
We ask this through our Lord, Jesus Christ, your Son
who lives and reigns with you and the Holy Spirit,
one God, forever and ever.
Amen.

(LIVING WATER PRAYERS OF OUR HERITAGE by Carl J. Pfeifer & Janaan Manternach, Paulist Press, pp. 78-79)

TO THINK AND TALK ABOUT

1. What was the answer Paulo Freire discovered to his question: "How can I help break the cycle of poverty that keeps people down?"
2. What new approach to the poor did Paulo Freire take?
3. Why was Paulo forced to leave his homeland?

TO READ AND ENJOY:

A Storybook:

THE LEGEND OF THE BLUEBONNET retold by Tomie de Paola (G. P. Putnam's Sons, 200 Madison Ave., New York, N.Y. 10016, 1983)

A Poem:

PAULO FREIRE

We can spell and write and read
And that is well and good.
But there are many who do not
Although they also could.
Paulo Freire found a way
And people learned to read.
And he will be remembered
Because he met this need.

(Promise, Poor, Recife, Depression, Systems, Brazil, Hungry, Homeland, Eleven, Freire

9

JEAN DONOVAN:
A Sensitive Conscience
1953-1980

Jean Donovan grew up in a suburb in Connecticut. Her parents loved her and gave her everything she needed. From the start Jean had almost anything any American child would want.

She loved life and had many interests. She studied hard and did well in school. She liked to have fun with her friends. She especially liked to ride horses.

When she grew up, Jean was very successful. She had a good job. She had her own apartment, a car, a motorcycle and nice clothes. She traveled to other countries. She had a boyfriend.

Jean seemed happy, but more and more she felt that her life was missing something important. She had everything she needed, but she slowly came to realize that many people had much less. She became aware of the real needs of others. Jean began to feel Christ calling her to do more for people in need.

Jean was now living in Cleveland. She decided to do volunteer work on Church projects. She found this satisfying, but still felt called to do more.

One day she read a story about El Salvador in Central America. The story told about people suffering from terrible poverty. They had little food, no decent places to live, few jobs and poor pay. They also feared for their lives, because many poor people just disappeared or were killed.

Jean learned that volunteers were needed to work with the poor peasants. Jean decided to go to El Salvador. She felt Christ calling her to reach out to people in so much pain.

She knew she would not have many things there that she took for granted in Cleveland. Her family and friends warned her of the dangers. But she volunteered and went to Central America.

What Jean saw in El Salvador was worse than she had imagined. She had never seen men, women and children so poor. She found it very hard to live in poverty with them. She felt sad that so many of the poor people had given up hope.

Jean worked with some American sisters who had been there longer. Together they did whatever they could to help suffering people. They worked with the poor to help them discover their own dignity as human beings. They also worked to change the conditions that caused their poverty and pain.

Jean soon realized that she and the sisters were in danger because of their work for the poor. She was often afraid, and at times wondered why she gave up such a pleasant life in Cleveland.

Her family, friends, and especially her boyfriend in Cleveland pleaded with her to come home before it was too late. They learned that two of Jean's friends were killed right outside the place where she lived.

But Jean felt that Christ wanted her to stay with the poor of El Salvador. She remembered how Jesus gave his whole life to help suffering people, especially people who were poor. So she stayed.

Jean Donovan and the sisters she worked with were shot to death on December 2, 1980. She was just twenty-seven years old.

JEAN DONOVAN

When the grid below is completed each pair of adjacent boxes will contain a two word answer. Clues are identified by the numbers in the boxes that correspond with the phrases below. The answer to 1-2 has been filled in as an example.

1	2	3	4
5	6	7	8
9	10	11	12
13	14	15	16
17	18	19	20

CLUES:

1- 2 The name of the person that the story is about
3- 4 The country where Jean worked with the poor
5- 6 The part of the world where El Salvador is
7- 8 The women Jean worked with to help the poor
9-10 The ones Jesus gave his whole life to help
11-12 Someone special that Jean left behind in Cleveland

13-14 The person Jean felt wanted her to stay with the poor
15-16 Where Jean grew up
17-18 Something Jean did when she was growing up that she especially enjoyed
19-20 Her age when she died

TO PRAY AND REMEMBER

Blessed art thou, Lord our God,
King of the Universe,
who has granted us life and sustenance
and permitted us to reach this day.

(The traditional prayer of thanksgiving, recited over the centuries.) LIVING WATER PRAYERS OF OUR HERITAGE by Carl J. Pfeifer & Janaan Manternach (Paulist Press, pp. 68-69)

TO THINK AND TALK ABOUT

1. Why did Jean Donovan leave her comfortable life in Cleveland?
2. What were some feelings that Jean experienced because of what she saw in El Salvador?
3. What motivated Jean to stay in El Salvador when it became so dangerous?

TO READ AND ENJOY:

A Storybook:

NADIA THE WILLFUL by Sue Alexander (Pantheon Books, Inc., 201 E. 50 St., New York, N.Y. 10022, 1983)

A Poem:

If someone has plenty
And another has none
Does someone share plenty
Or ignore the poor one?

Jean, Donovan, El, Salvador, Central, America, American, Sisters, Suffering, People, boy, friend, Jesus, Christ, Connecticut, Suburb, ride, horses, twenty, seven

11

ARCHBISHOP OSCAR ROMERO:

A Priest of Peace 1917-1980

He was a good priest. Fr. Romero was bright. He was honest. He prayed. He cared about people.

He knew that most of the people in his country, Salvador, were very poor. He was aware that half of the people of Salvador earned less than $10 a month. He knew, too, that most of the land was owned by a handful of very rich families.

As a good priest he helped rich and poor alike. He was kind and generous to the poor. He was popular among his fellow priests. His bishop liked him and named Father Romero his private secretary. He also put him in charge of the seminary where young men studied to become priests.

In 1970 the Pope named him a bishop. Seven years later the Pope named him Archbishop of San Salvador, the capital of his country.

Slowly Archbishop Romero changed. He listened to the priests of the diocese. He listened to poor farmers. He became more aware of the injustices in his country. He realized that the poor were poor because rich and powerful families kept them from owning land and earning enough money to live fuller lives.

Then something very tragic happened. More and more of his priests were being killed because they tried to help the poor struggle for justice. They were good priests. But they were put in jail and tortured. Or they were shot down in the streets by death squads.

Bishop Romero gradually stood up and spoke out for justice and against violence. He started a weekly radio program. Each Sunday he spoke of Christ's Gospel. He condemned the injustices that hurt the poor. He urged people to respect each other's rights and lives.

His weekly radio sermons became the most popular program in the country. Many poor families listened with earphones. They were afraid they would be tortured or killed if they were known to listen to Archbishop Romero's radio program.

The more popular Archbishop Romero became with the poor, the greater danger he was in. He regularly received threats of death. Even some of his fellow bishops disagreed with his strong statements. Many of the wealthy Catholics opposed him.

But he believed strongly that the Church must stand with the poor and speak up for their rights. Archbishop Romero began to speak out more clearly against the death squads. He spoke against the armed forces that seemed to be supporting those who killed innocent people. He spoke out against the government, challenging the leaders of his country to stop the violence and injustice.

He knew his life was in danger, but he continued to speak out—until March 24, 1980. At 6:30 that evening he was celebrating Mass in a hospital. Two men walked up to the altar after the homily. They shot the archbishop through the heart.

A fellow bishop called him "Saint Romero of the Americas."

OSCAR ROMERO

THE SPIRAL PUZZLE. Begin in the center of the puzzle with No. 1 and fill in the words moving clockwise, spiraling outward. See the clues below.

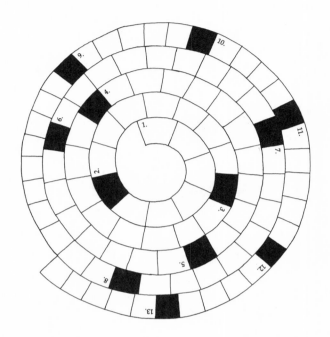

CLUES:
1. The last name of the person that the story is about
2. A need that he stood up and spoke out for
3. An evil that he stood up and spoke against
4. The poor were hurt by many of these
5. These were on the radio weekly and were very popular
6. People used these to listen to Romero's sermons
7. The name of his country
8. This was the title he had in San Salvador
9. He regularly received these kinds of threats
10. This is what he was celebrating when he was killed
11. This is the part of his body where the bullet went through
12. These are the people he died for
13. A fellow bishop called him this

TO PRAY AND REMEMBER

PSALM 18

I love you, O Lord, my strength,
O Lord, my rock, my fortress, my deliverer.
My God, my rock of refuge,
my shield, the horn of my salvation, my stronghold!
Praised be the Lord, I exclaim,
and I am safe from my enemies.

(Verses 1-4) (New American Bible)

TO THINK AND TALK ABOUT

1. What caused Archbishop Romero to slowly change?
2. What are some things that Archbishop Romero did that placed him in great danger?
3. How do you feel about the way Archbishop Romero lived out his life?

TO READ AND ENJOY:

A Storybook:

TWENTY AND TEN by Claire Huchet Bishop (Penguin Books, 625 Madison Ave., New York, N.Y. 10022, 1978)

A Poem:

ARCHBISHOP OSCAR ROMERO

In a corner of our world
A man stood up for right.
He spoke against the wrongs he saw
And worked with all his might.

He hated evils that he knew
His people suffered from.
And died because he wouldn't stop
Until his martyrdom.

Romero, Justice, Injustices, Sermons, Earphones, Salvador, Archbishop, Death, Mass, Heart, Poor, Saint

MARY McLEOD BETHUNE:
A Woman Who Helped People Read
1875-1955

This story is about Mary McLeod Bethune who was born more than 100 years ago in South Carolina—in the year 1875, as a matter of fact.

"Put that book down!" the little girl shouted at Mary. "Black people can't read."

Mary held the book carefully in her hands. All her life she wanted to learn to read.

She did not put the book down, but asked the two white girls, "You can read, can't you?"

"Of course we can read," one of them answered. "But you can't. So close that book and put it down!"

"Please show me how to read," Mary begged.

"We told you that black people can't read," one of the girls said nastily. "Go home now! Your mother is here with the laundry."

Mary's mother did the laundry for the family who lived on the big farm. She also cleaned their house.

Mary ran outside to wait for her mother. Tears filled her eyes. She sat down on the back steps and cried.

"What's wrong, child?" her mother asked when she came by. "Why are you crying?"

"They made me put their book down," Mary sobbed. "They said black people can't read. I want to read."

Mary's mother felt sad. She could not read. Mary's father couldn't read. Neither could any of her brothers and sisters. In fact Mary's mother didn't know any black people who could read.

"I am going to learn to read," Mary insisted as she and her mother walked home. "I don't know how, but I'm going to read someday."

Not long after, a church opened a school for black children. The teacher came to the cotton fields to find students. Mary's mother and father decided to let Mary go to the new school. Mary could hardly believe it. Her dream was going to come true.

Soon Mary could read. She read the Bible out loud in the evenings to her family. They were all very proud of her.

Mary did so well in the school that she was able to go on to a bigger school. She went to a Bible school in Chicago. The more Mary read the more she thought of her people in the cotton fields. "I want to help more of my people learn to read," she decided. So she became a teacher.

She started her own school for black children in Florida. She was a good teacher. She hired other good teachers. More and more children and young people came to her school. They all learned to read and to write. They also learned many other things.

Mary Bethune became well known for her work as a teacher. The President of the United States, Franklin D. Roosevelt, called her to Washington. He put her in charge of a national organization to help black people get better educations and better jobs. She was the first black woman to be in charge of a federal agency.

By the time she died thousands of her people were able to get good educations—all because one day the daughter of former slaves made up her mind that she would learn to read.

MARY McLEOD BETHUNE

Using the clues below, work the crossword puzzle.

DOWN:
1. Because of Mary, thousands of people were able to get a good_____.
3. Mary read the_____to her family.
4. Mary was from South_____.

ACROSS:
2. After Mary started school, her_____began to come true.
4. Mary went to a Bible school in_____.
5. Mary was a great_____.
6. In Florida, Mary started a_____for black children.
7. Mary was the_____black woman to be in charge of a federal agency.
8. Mary wanted to learn to_____.

TO PRAY AND REMEMBER

My God and Father,
without you I can do nothing;
with you I can do all
that you call me to do.
Help me.
Give me everything you know I need
to live and grow
and serve you.
With confidence I ask your help
in Jesus' name. Amen.

TO THINK AND TALK ABOUT

1. What did Mary Bethune decide that she was going to do?
2. How did Mary achieve her goal?
3. What are some things Mary did to help other people?

TO READ AND ENJOY:

A Storybook:

DOMINIC by William Steig (New York: Farrar, Straus, Giroux, 1972)

A Poem:

MARY McLEOD BETHUNE

She boldly said,
"I'll read someday,
I don't know how
But I'll find a way."

Her parents helped
Her dream come true
And as she read
Her dream grew, too:

To teach a school
And finally
Head of a
Federal Agency.

Education, Dream, Bible, Carolina, Chicago, Teacher, School, First, Read

LOUIS BRAILLE:
He Believed Blind People Could Read
1809-1852

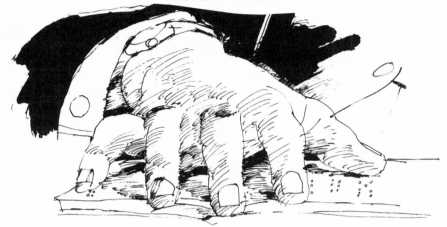

Louis Braille could not see. He was blind. But he could remember seeing people's faces and many colorful things.

He could see when he was a baby, until one very sad day. He was playing at home. He slipped or tripped. He fell on something sharp. It cut his eye. He screamed and cried.

His mother ran to him. She saw the cut. She picked up her screaming child and rushed to the doctors. But there was little they could do.

The pain was terrible. The wound became infected. The infection spread to both eyes. Soon he could not see at all. He was blind. He was just three years old.

Louis got used to stumbling over things and falling. He walked into people and things. His parents loved him very much. They patiently helped him learn to walk around the house without hurting himself.

As he grew up, his life became more and more lonely. He could go outside using a long white cane. But he could not play ball or any of the games the other children played.

He went to school, but fell behind. He could not read. So his parents sent him to a school for the blind when he was ten. This was better. He loved music. He learned to play the piano. But he still could not read. None of his blind classmates could read either.

Louis wanted to be able to read. He felt that there must be some way he and other blind people could read. They were as smart as anyone else. They just could not see. And because of that they were cut off from so much knowledge and beauty.

"Someday I will find a way to read," Louis told himself. "Then I can make it possible for all blind people to read."

When he was twelve, Louis started work on his dream. He thought and thought. He talked with his blind friends. He talked with his teachers. He found out that people had been trying for over a hundred years to find a way for blind persons to read. He became more convinced he had to find a way.

He started experimenting with a long pin and heavy paper. He punched holes in the paper. He tried hundreds of patterns. Nothing worked. People told him it was impossible. There was no way blind people could ever read books and newspapers. Some of his friends laughed at him as he kept punching holes in paper.

Louis would not give up. At times he got tired and discouraged, but for three years he spent most of his free time working on his invention. Then he found the key. He worked out an alphabet for the blind. Each letter was made of dots punched through heavy cardboard. The arrangement of the raised dots was different for each letter.

Now he could read. Now all blind people could learn to read using his alphabet of raised dots. Louis was fifteen years old.

People were excited about his discovery. They honored Louis by naming his alphabet after him. Blind people still use it and call it *braille*. Because of Louis they are able to read.

16

LOUIS BRAILLE

Find the twelve words hidden in the puzzle. They may
be vertical, horizontal, or diagonal. All the words are in
the story.

I	M	U	S	I	C	D	O	T	S
N	X	R	B	P	W	V	E	W	C
V	L	Q	U	R	W	B	R	E	F
E	X	D	R	E	A	M	V	L	I
N	F	G	J	H	K	I	B	V	F
T	R	S	P	T	V	W	L	E	T
I	E	L	V	X	Q	R	I	L	E
O	A	B	C	D	C	A	N	E	E
N	D	L	O	U	I	S	D	X	N

TO PRAY AND REMEMBER

PSALM 23

The Lord is my shepherd; I shall not want.
  In verdant pastures he gives me repose;
Beside restful waters he leads me;
  he refreshes my soul.
He guides me in right paths
  for his name's sake.
Even though I walk in the dark valley
  I fear no evil; for you are at my side
With your rod and your staff
  that give me courage.
You spread the table before me
  in the sight of my foes;
You anoint my head with oil;
  my cup overflows.
Only goodness and kindness follow me
  all the days of my life;
And I shall dwell in the house of the Lord
  for years to come.

(New American Bible)

TO THINK AND TALK ABOUT

1. What did Louis Braille want more than anything
   else?
2. How did Louis achieve his dream?
3. Why is Louis' invention so important?

TO READ AND ENJOY:

A Storybook:

THE SEEING STICK by Jane Yolen (Thomas Y.
Crowell Company, 666 Fifth Ave., New York, N.Y.
10019, 1977)

A Poem:

Dots into letters
To be touched by one's hand
Helps blind people read
All over this land.

(Louis, Braille, blind, alphabet, twelve, dots, read, fifteen,
invention, dream, music, cane)

17

JOAN OF ARC:
Following God's Call
1412-1431

Joan lived with her family on a small farm in France. They were poor. She worked in the fields and learned to sew and cook. She was not very pretty, but she was strong. She rode the farm horses better than her brothers. She loved to run races against the boys in her village. She usually won.

Then a terrible war changed everything. England invaded France. English armies roamed over the countryside, destroying crops and burning the homes of poor farmers.

Joan was just a teenager. She was thirteen when she felt that God was calling her to do something about the war.

It began one bright spring day. Joan was sitting in the pasture with her father's cows and sheep. She wondered why no one stood up to lead the French to fight against the British soldiers. She felt that God wanted her to get involved.

She talked to her father. He did not think war was something girls should take part in.

She talked to her pastor. He was more understanding. But he told her to pray more. She did pray more. And she became convinced that God was calling her to help save her country.

So she cut her long hair. She dressed in men's clothing. She rode with an escort of soldiers through enemy territory. She came to the palace of the prince. His name was Charles.

She went into the prince's palace. His guards led her to the prince. "God sent me to help you save our country," she told him. "God also wants me to help you become King of France."

Prince Charles laughed. So did everyone in the room. "How can a teenage farm girl help me win the war and save France?" he thought to himself. But after a while he decided to take Joan seriously.

"I will give you some soldiers," Prince Charles told her. "Your country will be thankful to you if you drive the English army out of France."

"That is what God is calling me to do," Joan said confidently.

So she led the soldiers into battle. They won a great victory at Orléans. The presence of this brave teenage girl, dressed in white armor, riding at the front of the soldiers, inspired everyone. Joan became a hero. And Prince Charles became King.

But then the army began to lose. Joan was captured by the English.

She was put in prison. People began to say she was a witch. Leaders of the Church illegally put her on trial. They tried to get her to admit that she practiced witchcraft. She denied the charge. She repeated that God called her to help save her country. "I cannot refuse God's call," she insisted. But she was condemned to death.

Joan was just nineteen when they executed her. It was a terrible mistake. The Church later realized she was a great young woman. We still honor her as St. Joan of Arc each May 30.

JOAN OF ARC

Unscramble the words below. All the words are in the story.

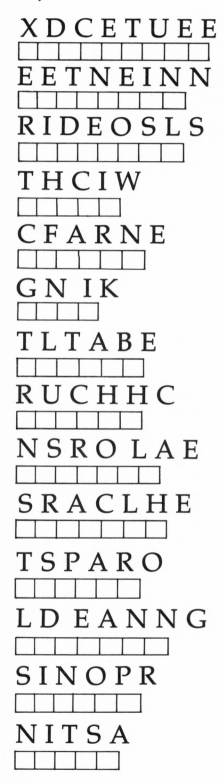

X D C E T U E E

E E T N E I N N

R I D E O S L S

T H C I W

C F A R N E

G N I K

T L T A B E

R U C H H C

N S R O L A E

S R A C L H E

T S P A R O

L D E A N N G

S I N O P R

N I T S A

TO PRAY AND REMEMBER

PRAYER TO ST. JOAN OF ARC

Most extraordinary soldier,
you insistently proclaimed;
"Let God be served first!"
You began by winning many victories
and received the plaudits of princes,
but then you were given to the enemy
and cruelly put to death.
Instill in us the desire to serve God first
and perform our earthly tasks with that idea
ever in our minds.

(NEW SAINT JOSEPH PEOPLE'S PRAYER BOOK #1073, p. 816)

TO THINK AND TALK ABOUT

1. What steps did Joan take to become a soldier?
2. How successful a soldier was Joan?
3. Why is Joan honored as a saint?

TO READ AND ENJOY:

A Storybook:

THE KISSIMMEE KID by Vera & Bill Cleaver (Bantam Books, Inc., 666 Fifth Ave., New York, N.Y., 10019)

A Poem:

JOAN OF ARC

Like Joan of Arc
God calls us, too
And we respond
By what we do.

We may not think
Of "call" each day
But who we are
Reveals God's way.

(executed, nineteen, witch, France, king, battle, church, Orleans, Charles, pastor, England, prison, saint)

ST. IGNATIUS LOYOLA:
In Search of Greatness
1491-1556

Ignatius was born in a castle. His parents were rich and powerful people in Loyola, a town in Spain.

Ignatius wanted to be great and famous. When he was young, he loved to read stories of great generals and kings. He enjoyed love stories in which a beautiful princess falls in love with a handsome knight.

As a young man, he seemed to live up to his dreams. He became a brave soldier. He went to war to defend his country. He fell in love with a beautiful princess. He hoped to win her love by his great bravery and strength.

Ignatius wanted fame. He wanted power. He wanted money. For him that is what made a person great.

All was going well for him, until one terrible day. He was leading a group of soldiers during a battle. A cannonball hit him in the leg. He was seriously hurt.

His friends carried him to a nearby castle. They laid him in bed. A doctor put his leg in a cast, but did a bad job. There were complications. The leg took a long time to heal. So Ignatius had to spend painful months in bed.

To take his mind off his pain, and to fill the empty days, Ignatius asked his friends for some books to read. He wanted to read his favorite kinds of stories, about wars and beautiful women. But they did not have any books like that in the castle.

They had only two books. One was a life of Jesus. The other told the stories of many saints. Ignatius began reading these books because there was nothing else to read.

Soon he began to feel a big change taking place inside him. He wanted even more than ever to become a great man. But reading about these great men and women saints made him change his ideas about greatness. He now wanted to be great the way St. Francis or St. Dominic were great.

Ignatius read how Jesus and the saints became great by doing whatever God wanted them to do. They prayed. They reached out to help other people, especially people who were suffering. They were more concerned with helping the little people of the world than with becoming great and famous.

Ignatius decided that when his leg was healed, he would do even greater things than the saints had done. He would change his whole life. He would live more to help people see how great God is rather than to say how great Ignatius is. Instead of fame, power and money Ignatius now wanted to be more like Jesus.

It was a hard struggle, but Ignatius changed. He made some good friends who shared his new ideal of greatness. They also wanted to find greatness in loving God and other people. The Pope allowed Ignatius and his friends to become a community called the Society of Jesus, or Jesuits. They took as a motto: "All for the greater glory of God."

Ignatius became great—a great Christian, a saint. We celebrate his feastday each July 31.

ST. IGNATIUS OF LOYOLA

THE SPIRAL PUZZLE. Begin in the center with No. 1 and fill in the words moving clockwise, spiraling outward. See the clues below.

CLUES:
1. The name of the saint who started the Society of Jesus
2. The town where Ignatius was born
3. The country where Ignatius was born
4. The profession Ignatius chose as a young man
5. The person whose life he read while he was hospitalized
6. Great men and women he also read about while he was hospitalized
7. Another name for the Society of Jesus
8. This is what reading about great men and women saints made him do about his ideas of greatness
9 & 10. Two saints that he wanted to be like
11. Another word that is almost the same as Society
12. "All for the greater glory of God" is the _____of the Jesuits
13. This is what Ignatius became
14. The month in which his feastday is celebrated

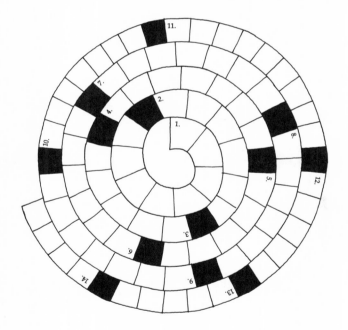

TO PRAY AND REMEMBER

PRAYER OF ST. IGNATIUS OF LOYOLA

Teach us, Lord,
  to serve you
    as you deserve;
to give
  and not to count the cost;
to fight
  and not to heed the wounds;
to toil
  and not to ask for rest;
to labor
  and not to ask for any reward,
  save that of knowing
    that we do your will,
    through Jesus Christ
      our Lord. Amen.

(LIVING WATER PRAYERS OF OUR HERITAGE by Carl J. Pfeifer & Janaan Manternach (Paulist Press), p. 47)

TO THINK AND TALK ABOUT

1. When Ignatius was a young man what did he think made a person great?
2. How were Ignatius' ideas about greatness changed?
3. How did Ignatius become truly great?

TO READ AND ENJOY:

A Storybook:

THE CROSSROAD CHILDREN'S BIBLE (The Crossroad Publishing Company, 575 Lexington Avenue, New York, N.Y., 10022) and/or THE SAINT BOOK by Kate Dooley (Paulist Press)

A Poem:

I do not know
What I will be.
My dreams for now
Are fantasies.

But I believe
That I will be
The most that God
Has planned for me

Ignatius, Loyola, Spain, Soldier, Jesus, Saints, Jesuits, Change, Francis, Dominic, Community, Motto, Saint, July

MOTHER TERESA:
The Angel of Calcutta 1910-

Agnes grew up on a small farm in Yugoslavia. She was strong, healthy and a hard worker.

She loved her parents and her brother and sister. She loved her home.

In school Agnes heard about India. She learned of the missionaries who worked there in the city of Calcutta. When she was twelve, she wanted to become a missionary and go to India. She felt that God was calling her to become a nun, a religious sister.

For six years the desire to be a nun and go to India grew. When Agnes was eighteen, she left home to become a Sister of Loreto. She knew they had missions in India.

Agnes became Sister Teresa. She was sent to a convent in India.

Sister Teresa loved being a nun. She loved being a teacher in the Loreto school in Calcutta. She loved the girls she taught and they loved her.

The school and convent were large and beautiful. They were in a nice part of the city, and had a lovely garden. Sister Teresa was very happy. She taught there for almost twenty years. For some of the time she was principal of the school.

During those years Sister Teresa learned how poor many people in India were. One day she was riding a train to another city. As she rode along, she felt that God was calling her to do more for the poor of Calcutta.

She decided to leave the Sisters of Loreto. She wanted to live and work with the poorest people in the city. She wrote to the Pope and asked permission to leave the Sisters of Loretto. The Pope gave his permission.

So Sister Teresa moved out of the comfortable convent and moved into the slums of Calcutta. She learned how to help sick people. She started her own school for poor children. At first there were just five children. But more and more poor children came to her school.

Some of the girls she taught at the Loretto school came to help her. They formed a new religious community, called the Missionary Sisters of Charity. Sister Teresa came to be known as Mother Teresa.

She and her young Sisters knew that many poor people lived and died in the streets and alleys of the crowded city. One day Mother Teresa found a dying woman in the street. She picked her up and carried her to a hospital.

Mother Teresa decided to open a home for poor dying street people. She and her sisters opened a Home for the Dying. They went out and carried dying men and women to their Home. They cared for them.

More and more young women joined Mother Teresa and her community. They wanted to live with and for the very poorest of the poor. They wanted to be like Mother Teresa.

Mother Teresa is now known all over the world. She won the Nobel Peace Prize. Many people call her a living saint.

MOTHER TERESA

TWO WORD PUZZLE. When the grid below is completed each pair of adjacent boxes will contain a two word answer. Clues are identified by the numbers in the boxes that correspond with the phrases below.

1- 2. A place in Yugoslavia where Agnes grew up
3- 4. The city where Agnes wanted to go when she was twelve
5- 6. This is what Agnes felt God was calling her to become
7- 8. The number of years she desired to become a nun
9-10. The school in Calcutta where she taught
11-12. The number of years she taught and was principal
13-14. The people she started a school for in the slums of Calcutta
15-16. This is what she formed with some girls who came to the Calcutta slums to help her
17-18. The name Sister Teresa became known as
19-20. This is what many people call her

1.	2.	3.	4.
5.	6.	7.	8.
9.	10.	11.	12.
13.	14.	15.	16.
17.	18.	19.	20.

TO PRAY AND REMEMBER

THE LORD'S PRAYER

Our Father
Who art in heaven,
Hallowed be thy name.
Thy kingdom come,
Thy will be done
On earth as it is in heaven.
Give us this day
Our daily bread;
And forgive us our trespasses
As we forgive those
Who trespass against us;
And lead us not into temptation,
But deliver us from evil.
Amen!

(LIVING WATER PRAYERS OF OUR HERITAGE by Carl J. Pfeifer & Janaan Manternach, p. 33)

TO THINK AND TALK ABOUT

1. How did a young woman from Yugoslavia end up in the slums of Calcutta, India?
2. What motivated Mother Teresa to open a Home for the Dying?
3. How has Mother Teresa been rewarded for the things she has done?

Small, Farm, Calcutta, India, Religious, Sister, six, years, Loreto, school, twenty, years, poor, children, Religious, community, Mother, Teresa, living, Saint

TO READ AND ENJOY:

A Storybook:

MAMA'S GOING TO BUY YOU A MOCKING BIRD by Jean Little (Viking Penguin Inc., 40 West 23rd Street, New York, N.Y. 1984)

A Poem:

MOTHER TERESA OF CALCUTTA

Here breathes
A woman
Unafraid
To do what
Needs be done.
She finds
A way in
Every place
Beneath the
Rising sun
To feed
The hungry
Aid the sick
Bring peace
To those
Who die.
And in
Her homes
For orphans
Love heeds
A baby's cry.

ST. JOHN BOSCO:
Finding A Better Way
1815-1888

One day John saw some boys and girls fighting. They were yelling at one another. They called each other names. They were hitting and kicking and pulling one another's hair.

John was afraid to go near them, but he had to get home. So he tried to run by.

But there was no way around the angry gang. So he pulled one of the boys out of the way and tried to run past them all.

"Hey, you!" yelled the boy whom John pushed. "Who do you think you are pushing around?"

He swung at John and hit him on the chest. John tried to tell them to stop fighting. They did stop hitting one another long enough to gang up on John.

They called him names. They pulled his hair. They tore his clothes. They kicked and hit him. Then they laughed at him.

They finally let John go. He ran toward home. Halfway down the street he stopped and turned around to look back at the violent gang that beat him up. They were back to fighting with one another.

John opened the door to his house. His mother was shocked at the sight of him. Blood and bruises covered his face. His shirt was in shreds. "John," she cried, "what happened to you?"

John told her about the rough gang that was fighting in the street. "There must be a better way to have fun," John's mother said sadly.

A few days later John went with his mother to the farmer's market. It was crowded. It was exciting. John was captivated by a show being held in the marketplace. There were jugglers and acrobats and magicians. John had never seen anything like it.

"I bet I could learn to do that," he said to himself as he watched the juggler. "And that, too," as he enjoyed the acrobats. "And even that," he said as the magician did his tricks.

Back at home John set out to learn to do what the show people did. He practiced every moment he could in between school and chores. Soon he was good enough to put on a show of his own.

"Maybe I can help the boys and girls find a better way to have fun than to fight all the time," John thought.

He called out, "Come see the greatest show on earth!" The rough boys and girls came out of curiosity. But they threatened to beat up John if they didn't like his show.

John juggled balls and plates. He stood on his head and did somersaults. He walked on a tightrope. He did magic tricks.

The children laughed and clapped. They liked what John was doing. He even taught them some of his tricks. They began to practice. They wanted to be able to do what John did.

John told them stories. He made some up. He took some from the Bible. The children loved to hear John's stories.

When he grew up, John kept doing his juggling and acrobatics and magic tricks. He continued to tell stories. He even started a school for children. He helped them find a better way to live than by violence and fighting. We know him as St. John Bosco and celebrate his feast on January 31.

SAINT JOHN BOSCO

MATCHING WORDS AND COMPLETING PHRASES.
Find in the story words that complete a phrase or match a
word.

1. farmer's	(market)
2. market	(place)
3. juggled	(balls or plates)
4. magic	(tricks)
5. John	(Bosco)
6. violent	(gang)
7. tight	(rope)
8. name	(calling)
9. show	(people)
10. Bible	(stories)

TO PRAY AND REMEMBER

Lord, grant me
the serenity to accept the things
I cannot change,
the courage to change the things
I can,
and the wisdom
to know the difference.

(LIVING WATER PRAYERS OF OUR HERITAGE by Carl J.
Pfeifer & Janaan Manternach (Paulist Press, p. 55)

TO THINK AND TALK ABOUT

1. What inspired John to juggle and do magic tricks?
2. How did John get the boys and girls in his village to do something other than fight?
3. What did John do when he grew up?

TO READ AND ENJOY:

A Storybook:

THE BULLY OF BARKHAM STREET by Mary
Stolz (Harper & Row Publishers, 10 E. 53 St., New
York, N.Y. 10022, 1980)

A Poem:

You chipped at me
By what you said.
It hurt so much
I wished you dead.

I know that
I've done mean things, too
But we were friends
Just me and you.

I wonder what
It means to be
Good friends and
Then an enemy?

FLANNERY O'CONNOR:
An Imaginative Writer
1925-1964

in that house. Her great-grandmother donated the land for the first church in Milledgeville.

There she began to write. She loved to write. She had a vivid imagination. She tried to write about her experiences of life, and about what she saw in the world around her. She tried to write what she believed most deeply.

She did not write theology or philosophy. She wrote short stories and novels. They were filled with a vision of life drawn from her Catholic faith.

She was a born story teller. And she worked very hard to write well. She studied creative writing at the University of Iowa. Her writings began to be known and appreciated. She became known as Flannery O'Connor rather than as Mary.

A famous author invited her to spend time as a guest of his family in Connecticut. She accepted the invitation. She wrote some of her best works there. During her stay she began her days with Mass every morning at a church four miles away.

Then she began to feel pains in her bones. Her father had died of a bone disease. She feared she had the same incurable illness. She was right. She spent months in the hospital.

Finally she was able to return to Milledgeville. She faced her pain bravely. She continued to write. She became more and more famous for her novels and short stories.

People were impressed with Flannery O'Connor's skill and imagination as a writer. But they were as much impressed with her faith as a Catholic.

She kept beside her typewriter a Bible, a Sunday Missal and a Breviary. She read and prayed from them frequently. She prayed often while she wrote. Her faith deepened as she struggled with the disease she knew would eventually kill her.

Flannery O'Connor used her imagination and her creative skills as a writer to share with the world a vision of faith and hope. Even after she had to use crutches to get around she continued to write stories that helped people believe in God's love in a world filled with pain and evil.

Flannery O'Connor received many awards as a great writer. She was invited to teach others the art of writing. At her death people mourned the loss of a great writer. Her stories grew out of her rich experience of life and her deep Catholic faith. She had found beauty and Christ in the midst of suffering and evil.

Mary grew up in Savannah, Georgia. Her father was a real estate agent. She learned what it meant to be a Catholic by growing up in a Catholic family in a city where there were few Catholics.

She went to parochial school. There she learned more about life and about Catholic teachings. She began to believe that Jesus Christ and the Catholic Church had much to say about life.

When she was thirteen, her family moved from Savannah to her grandmother's home in the town of Milledgeville, Georgia. It became a very special place for Mary. A century before one of the few priests in Georgia had celebrated Mass regularly

FLANNERY O'CONNOR

Unscramble the words below. All the words are in the story.

L L L L D M E E I I G E V

Y E A F N N R L

T O H C L C A I

T C T C N O N I E C U

V Y B I A E R R

A R E G O I G

W A O I

R T S O E I S

E L I B B

R T T Y E W R P E I

T R E W I R

D A A R S W

A L S S I M

L O V E N S

PSALM 31

In you, O Lord, I take refuge;
    let me never be put to shame.
In your justice rescue me,
    incline your ear to me,
    make haste to deliver me!
Be my rock of refuge,
    a stronghold to give me safety.
You are my rock and my fortress;
    for your name's sake you will lead and guide me.

(Verses 2-4)

TO THINK AND TALK ABOUT

1. How did Mary (Flannery O'Connor) learn what being a Catholic meant?
2. What kind of writing did Mary (Flannery O'Connor) do?
3. What was there about Flannery O'Connor that impressed people?

TO READ AND ENJOY:

A Storybook:

EMMA by Wendy Kesselman (Harper & Row, 10 E. 53 ST., New York, N.Y. 10022, 1980)

A Poem:

FLANNERY O'CONNOR

She wrote the stories
That she knew
And as she lived
The stories grew.

They spoke of hope,
Of faith, of pain,
Of love and death,
Of loss and gain.

She wrote the stories
That she knew
And as she wrote
Her beauty grew.

(Milledgeville, Catholic, Connecticut, Breviary, Georgia, Iowa, stories, Bible, typewriter, writer, awards, Missal, novels)

GERARD MANLEY HOPKINS, S.J.:
A Poet
1844-1889

He remembered how his father read the poems aloud to the family on special occasions.

Gerard remembered, too, how he wrote poems as a child. Some of them were good. He even won a prize for a poem he wrote in high school. Now all his poems were being eaten by the flames.

Gerard Manley Hopkins threw himself into his studies. He also spent some time as a teacher, something he found very hard. He gave up poetry as a distraction from his vocation as a Jesuit. Besides he did not think his poems were all that good.

But his feelings slowly changed. The more he studied about God, and the more of life he experienced, the more he sensed God's presence in the world around him. He felt God with him as he enjoyed a beautiful sunset. He found God even in his problems and struggles.

Then one day there was a terrible tragedy. A German ship ran aground during a storm. Wind and waves battered the ship for a day and a night. Sixty people drowned. Gerard's sensitive heart was touched by the horror. Could God be found even there?

Gerard's superiors urged him to write a poem about the tragedy. He did. He wrote "The Wreck of the Deutschland." He knew now that poetry was not a distraction from his life as a Jesuit priest. He began to write poems again.

He wrote of God's presence with us everywhere. "The world is charged with the grandeur of God," he began one poem. It summed up his experience as a poet and his beliefs as a Jesuit. He mailed copies of his poems as he wrote them to a poet friend, Robert Bridges.

But no one would publish his poetry. Gerard kept writing, despite his discouragement. He continued to work hard as a priest with Irish immigrants, and as a teacher, until he died of typhoid at age 44. His last words were, "I am so happy. I am so happy."

Twenty years later his friend, Robert Bridges, had Gerard Manley Hopkins' poems published. People came to recognize him as one of the finest poets of the English language. His poetry continues to help people sense God's presence in their lives.

Gerard placed two more logs on the fireplace in his room. He watched as the flames leapt up and licked at the metal grate. Slowly, deliberately he gathered up all the pages of his poetry. He paused for a moment, holding his poems, gazing at the fire. Then he quickly placed the papers in the fire. He sat down and watched his poems, the work of years, turn into ashes.

"My poetry must never come between me and God," he thought to himself. "I must give myself completely to God in my new life as a Jesuit. There will be no time for poetry as a priest."

As he stared at the flames dancing through the blackened papers, he looked back over the years to his boyhood home in Stratford, England. As long as he could remember poetry was a big part of his life.

His father, Manley Hopkins, wrote poetry at home after working all day at his insurance office.

GERARD MANLEY HOPKINS

THE SPIRAL PUZZLE. Begin in the center with No. 1 and fill in the words moving clockwise, spiraling outward. See the clues below.

CLUES:
1. The first name of the poet that the story is about
2. His father's first name and the poet's second name
3. Their family name
4. Something that both he and his father wrote
5. The religious order that he joined
6. One of the things that he was that he found very hard
7. The more he studied about God the more he sensed this in the world around him (2 words)
8. The name of the poem that he wrote about a terrible tragedy (5 words)
9. The disease that he died from
10. People recognized him as one of the great_____ of the English language

TO PRAY AND REMEMBER

PRAYER OF THANKSGIVING

Blessed art thou, Lord our God,
King of the universe,
who has granted us life and sustenance
and permitted us to reach this day.

(LIVING WATER PRAYERS OF OUR HERITAGE by Carl J. Pfeifer & Janaan Manternach (Paulist Press, pp. 68-69)

TO THINK AND TALK ABOUT

1. Why did Gerard burn his poetry before he became a Jesuit?
2. What changed his feelings about being a poet?
3. What did Gerard do when no one would publish his poetry?

TO READ AND ENJOY:

A poetry book:

BY MYSELF by Lee Bennett Hopkins (Thomas Y. Crowell, 10 E. 53 St., New York, N.Y., 10022, 1980)

A Poem:

GERARD MANLEY HOPKINS

His poems spoke of wonder
And God's presence everywhere,
In sunsets and in struggles,
In tragedy and care.

Gerard Manley Hopkins
Was an artist without fame
Till after death his poems
Brought him much deserved acclaim.

Key: 1. Gerard 2. Manley 3. Hopkins 4. poetry 5. Jesuit 6. teacher 7. God's presence 8. The Wreck of the Deutschland 9. typhoid 10. poets

ST. JANE FRANCES
de CHANTAL:
A Brave Widow
1572-1641

Jane Frances' mother died when she was only 18 months old. Her father, an important political leader in France, raised his daughter. He saw to it that she received an excellent education from tutors who taught her at home. She grew up to be a beautiful, sensitive woman, cheerful and full of life. Her father was the biggest influence in her life until she married.

When Jane Frances was twenty-one she met a nobleman, Baron Christophe de Chantal. They grew to love one another and were soon married. They lived together in his castle.

They had six children, but two of them died as infants. Christophe was often away, serving in the king's army. Jane Frances raised the children and also managed the castle. She had to supervise the work in the fields as well as inside the castle.

Jane Frances was good to the servants and workers. She was very generous to the poor who came to the castle for something to eat. She was particularly kind to people who were sick or elderly.

The happiest days for Jane Frances were when Christophe was home with her. They were happily married for seven years. Then Christophe was killed in a hunting accident.

That sad moment changed Jane Frances' life. She was now alone, a young widow. She had four young children to care for. Jane became very depressed. She wondered how she could go on alone. For four months she could hardly cope with it all.

Christophe's father was very angry with his daughter-in-law. He demanded that Jane Frances and the children live with him. He threatened to disinherit the children if they did not live in his home. His housekeeper did not want Jane and the children there. She made life difficult for them.

Jane struggled cheerfully to make the best of a difficult situation. She missed her husband terribly. She taught her children to read and to count. She also taught them their prayers. She took good care of them.

One day she met a great and holy priest, Francis de Sales. They became friends. She shared with him her problems and her hopes. He helped her see God at work in her life. Francis told her of one of his dreams.

He wanted to bring together young girls and widows to form a new kind of religious community. They would live together, praying and working. But they would not stay inside the convent like other religious women. They would go out to visit the sick and poor in their homes.

Jane Frances felt God calling her to that kind of life. Her children were grown. One was already married. After much thought and prayer Jane Frances decided to begin a new life as a nun.

She became one of the first Visitation Sisters. She lived the rest of her life with the other sisters, working, praying, and caring for others. St. Francis de Sales said of her, "She was one of the holiest people I ever met." The Church honors her as a saint, celebrating her feast every December 12.

JANE FRANCES de CHANTAL

MATCHING or MEANING. Find in the story words that match or mean the same thing as the clue word.

1. Jane	(Frances)
2. house	(keeper)
3. Visitation	(Sisters)
4. new	(life)
5. political	(leader)
6. noble	(man)
7. nun	(sister)
8. Francis	(de Sales)
9. religious	(community of women)
10. teachers	(tutors)
11. palace	(castle)
12. sad	(depressed)

TO PRAY AND REMEMBER

PRAYER TO KNOW THE WILL OF GOD

Lord,
what is your will that I do?
I am completely open to your plan for me.
I desire to live only in you
and to be guided by you forever.
Grant that your holy will
may be carried out perfectly in me.
St. Jane Frances de Chantal (1572-1641)

(The above prayer is in the NEW SAINT JOSEPH PEOPLE'S PRAYER BOOK, #512, p. 411)

TO THINK AND TALK ABOUT

1. What was Jane Frances' life like when she was growing up?
2. How did Jane Frances live her life as the wife of a baron?
3. How did she live her life after her husband's death?

TO READ AND ENJOY:

A Storybook:

SARAH, PLAIN AND TALL by Patricia MacLachlan (Harper & Row Junior Books, 10 East 53rd Street, New York, N.Y. 10022, 1985)

A Poem:

JANE FRANCES de CHANTAL

God was with
Jane Frances
Through her
Struggles and
Her strife.
And through it all
Jane Frances
Made a saint
Out of
Her life.

ST. ISIDORE:
A Simple Farmer 1070-1130

Isidore grew up in a small village just outside Madrid in Spain. His family was very poor. From the time he was a young boy he had to work in the fields to help his mother and father. There was no time or money for Isidore to go to school. He probably never learned to read or write.

From the time he was a boy until he died Isidore worked on the farm of a rich landowner, Juan de Varga. He never had a chance to see more of the world than his village and the nearby city of Madrid. He worked hard in the fields all his life.

When he was a young man, Isidore married a young woman as poor and uneducated as he was. He and Maria loved each other very much. They had little more than what they needed to live the simplest of lives. But they were very happy.

They were overjoyed when Maria knew she would have a baby. One of the happiest days of their lives was when their son was born. But their joy soon turned to sadness. Their only son died as a very young child. Isidore and Maria were not able to have any other children.

Isidore worked in the fields from sunrise to sundown. Maria took care of their small house. They went to Mass each morning before Isidore went out to the farm. They prayed together every morning and evening. On Sundays they often took walks through the great city of Madrid, stopping at the many churches in the city.

Isidore loved nature. He noticed everything as he walked behind his plow or worked with his hoe. He loved the feel and smell of newly plowed earth. He rejoiced at the first signs of green sprouting from the ground in spring. Everything reminded him of God, who creates the world and all that is in it. He found it easy to talk with God during the day as he worked in the hot sun or rested in the cool shade.

The landowner for whom he worked all his life admired Isidore and his wife. Juan de Varga had money, education, a big house with many servants, large farms with many workers, and an important place in the world. But he felt that Isidore and Maria were happier than he was, and more generous. The two shared the little that they had with people even poorer than they were.

Isidore's fellow workers liked and respected him because he was not only a good worker but a very caring man. Their one complaint was that from time to time Isidore came late to work from church.

As the years wore on, Isidore and his wife grew older. They continued to work, but could not work the long hours they once did. They prayed more and shared more with others and enjoyed being with their many friends.

When he and Maria died, people were very sad. They not only loved this farm worker and his wife, but they felt they were very holy. The Church honors Isidore and Maria as saints. Isidore is called the patron of farmers. He is also patron of the National Rural Life Conference of the United States. His feastday is May 15.

ST. ISIDORE the FARMER

Find the 12 words hidden in the puzzle. They may be vertical,
horizontal or diagonal. All the words are in the story.

J	X	L	B	T	P	A	T	R	O	N
Z	U	N	A	T	U	R	E	M	W	X
T	F	A	R	M	E	R	S	L	Q	M
P	L	A	N	D	O	W	N	E	R	A
X	P	L	W	D	Q	O	C	D	Y	D
S	Z	R	I	T	E	L	B	F	G	R
M	A	S	S	H	W	V	X	R	C	I
Q	I	M	P	Z	N	Y	A	L	F	D
T	Z	W	A	P	C	H	U	R	C	H
X	L	G	I	H	M	N	O	P	G	Q
S	A	I	N	T	S	M	A	R	I	A

TO PRAY AND REMEMBER

PRAYER TO ST. ISIDORE the FARMER

Dear Isidore,
you know how normal it is to cultivate the land
for you were employed as a farm laborer
for the greater part of your life,
Although you received God's help materially
through angels in the field,
All farmers are aided spiritually
to see the wonders God has strewn on this earth.
Encourage all farmers in their labors
and help them to feed numerous people.

(NEW SAINT JOSEPH PEOPLE'S PRAYER BOOK, #1018,
p. 789)

TO THINK AND TALK ABOUT

1. How is your childhood like or different from
   Isidore's and Maria's?
2. How are your parents' lives like or different from
   Isidore's and Maria's?

3. Why do you believe the Church honors Isidore
   and Maria as saints?

TO READ AND ENJOY:

A Storybook:

NATURAL HISTORY by M. B. Goffstein (Farrar,
Straus, & Giroux, Inc., 19 Union Square W., New
York, N.Y. 10003, 1979)

A Poem:

ISIDORE and MARIA

They prayed
And helped
Where there
Was need.
Their simple lives
Were great
In deed.

Key: patron, Juan de Varga, farmers, Isidore, Madrid, Maria,
saints, nature, Spain, Mass, landowner, church

EVE LAVALLIERE:
A Great Actress
1866-1929

Eve Lavalliere was born in a small town in France about 120 years ago. Her father was a violent man who often drank too much. When he was drunk, he beat Eve's mother. He even threatened his little daughter. Many times Eve and her mother ran from the house and took a train to the home of relatives.

As a child Eve was mostly sad and lonely. She felt that neither her mother nor her father loved her as much as they loved her brother.

She looked forward to going to school. But she found little love from her teachers or from her fellow students.

By the time she was ten Eve felt very badly about herself. Her parents sent her off to another school further from home. Here Eve felt loved for the first time. She received her First Communion. She began to blossom.

After finishing school, Eve returned home. She found some happiness in acting. She started a group of teenage actors.

But her home situation kept getting worse. When Eve was 17, her mother left her father. Eve went to live with her mother. One evening her father visited them. There was an angry fight. The father pulled out a gun, shot Eve's mother, and was about to shoot Eve, but shot himself instead.

Eve was just 18, and was now an orphan. She became very depressed. She thought of suicide.

Then she met a rich man who invited Eve to join his group of actors and actresses. They trav-eled around to small towns putting on plays. Eve loved to act and was good at it.

She moved to Paris. There she began to become known as a very good actress. She worked hard and after some years became a great star. She was one of the most famous actresses in Paris.

She lived very well. She had plenty of money. She was very successful. She was beautiful. Many men loved her. All Paris loved her. She seemed to have everything.

But she still felt lonely and sad. She felt something was missing. She again thought of suicide. In fact she tried three times to end her life.

In 1917 she was invited to come to the United States to act. Before leaving for America, Eve decided to take a long vacation in a quiet village in the French countryside.

There she accidently met the village priest. He asked her why she never came to Mass. At first Eve laughed at him. Then she argued with him. They often walked and talked together. One day she realized that it was God she was missing in her life. She decided to change her whole life.

She gave up her riches and her fame as a star. She became a Third Order Franciscan and went to Africa to care for poor, sick children. She had to return to France because of her own poor health.

Eve lived a very simple life after that. She prayed much and helped others however she could. She was often sick and suffered much. But she had found peace in loving God and other people. After much suffering Eve died in 1929.

EVE LAVALLIERE

Using the clues below, work the crossword puzzle.

DOWN
1. The country where Eve was born
2. What Eve became at the age of 18
4. The country that invited her to come and act in 1917 (two words)
5. The number of times she tried to end her life
6. The city where she was one of the most famous actresses
10. Something Eve was that she gave up being
12. A word to describe a small section of a country

ACROSS
1. A Third Order that Eve joined
3. Something Eve loved to do
7. The country where she cared for poor, sick children
8. A word that describes how both of Eve's parents died
9. Something Eve tried three times
11. Something that a priest asked her why she never attended
13. The name of the person the story is about (2 words)
14. The title of a person who inspired Eve to change her whole life
15. Who Eve found was missing in her life

TO PRAY AND REMEMBER

ACT OF FAITH

My God, I place my life in your hands.
I trust you fully,
because I know you love me and care for me.
I believe you are always with me.
I open my mind to your Word
and my heart to your call.
With the aid of your Holy Spirit,
help me grow in faith
as I grow in age and experience.
I ask this in Jesus' name. Amen.

(LIVING WATER PRAYERS OF OUR HERITAGE by Carl J. Pfeifer & Janaan Manternach, Paulist Press, p. 42)

TO THINK AND TALK ABOUT

1. How is your life as a child different from or the same as Eve's?
2. How did Eve live out a large part of her life?
3. Why and how did Eve change her whole life?

TO READ AND ENJOY:

A Storybook:

THE STORY OF JUMPING MOUSE by John Steptoe (Lothrop, Lee & Shepard Books, 105 Madison Ave., New York, N.Y. 10016, 1984)

A Poem:

EVE LAVALLIERE

Lovely as an actress,
Often very sad.
Seeming to have everything
Didn't make her glad.

In a quiet village
Her need for God she found.
Gave away her riches
And turned her life around.

France, Franciscan, Orphan, Act, United States, Three, Paris, Africa, Shot, Suicide, Star, Mass, Village, Eve Lavalliere, Priest, God

THOMAS MERTON:
A Monk for the World
1915-1968

He traveled with his father all over Europe. For a while Tom studied in England. He read about the great leader in India, Mahatma Gandhi. Tom was very impressed with Gandhi's love for the poor and his love for peace. Tom was surprised to read that Gandhi admired Jesus and studied the Gospels.

When Tom was sixteen, his father died of a brain tumor. Tom felt all alone. He went to Italy. He loved the paintings and statues all over Rome. He began to read the Bible so he could learn about the people and stories he saw in the art of Italy.

Then he decided to go back to the United States. He studied at Columbia University in New York. Tom was sad to see the many poor people in the streets of New York. He wanted to find ways to help them.

So he studied hard. He read all the time. He wanted to be a newspaper reporter, a writer. He felt that he could help others by what he wrote. But his life was not all that happy. He felt that something important was missing, but he didn't know just what it was.

Then his grandfather died. Tom loved him very much. As he looked at his grandfather's body, Tom began to pray. He felt a great need for God. It was God that was missing from his life.

After that Tom prayed more. He read religious books. Once he dropped into a Catholic church for Sunday Mass. Soon he decided to become a Catholic.

He was baptized when he was 23. He thought now about being a priest. He visited the Trappist monastery in Gethsemani, Kentucky. There he felt a great peace and joy. He decided to become a Trappist monk.

In the monastery Tom had time to write. He wrote books that millions of people read. He helped thousands of people find God. He wrote about the poor, and about peace. He wrote against war. He became very famous for his writings.

He was concerned about everything happening in the world, but he spent his life in the quiet of the Trappist monastery. He knew that he belonged there, where he could spend his life praying and writing. When he died accidently, many people said they were sure Thomas Merton was a saint.

Tom was born in France. But he grew up in New York. His mother and father were artists.

His mother taught him to read and to love books. She took him with her to church on Sunday. She was a Quaker. Tom's father did not go to church.

Tom's mother died of cancer before he was ten. His father took Tom with him to France. It was exciting at first. But it was hard, too.

They lived in a French village. The village was built around the church. All the streets led to the church. Almost everyone was Catholic. Tom felt like an outsider. He spent much time reading books of all kinds. He began to want to be a writer.

1.	2.
3.	4.
5.	6.
7.	8.
9.	10.
11.	12.
13.	14.
15.	16.
17.	18.
19.	20.

THOMAS MERTON

TWO WORD PUZZLE. When the grid below is completed each pair of adjacent boxes will contain a two word answer. Clues are identified by the numbers in the boxes that correspond with the phrases below.

CLUES:
1- 2 The name of the person that the story is about
3- 4 A school where he studied
5- 6 One of the things that he wanted to be was a_____
7- 8 A place he went to for Sunday Mass
9-10 The city in which he grew up
11-12 After he left Italy he lived in the_____
13-14 He eventually became a_____
15-16 He was very impressed with the great Indian leader_____
17-18 He spent his life in the quiet of a_____
19-20 His monastery was in_____

TO PRAY AND REMEMBER

THE ROAD AHEAD

My Lord God,
I have no idea where I am going.
I do not see the road ahead of me.
I cannot know for certain where it will end.
Nor do I really know myself,
and the fact that I think that I am following your will does not mean that I am actually doing so.
But I believe that the desire to please you does in fact please you.

And I hope I have that desire in all that I am doing.
I hope that I will never do anything apart from that desire.
And I know that if I do this,
you will lead me by the right road though I may know nothing about it.
Therefore will I trust you always
though I may seem to be lost and in the shadow of death.
I will not fear, for you are ever with me,
and you will never leave me to face my perils alone.

Thomas Merton (1915-1968)

(The above prayer was taken from LORD, HEAR OUR PRAYER compiled by Thomas McNally, C.S.C. Ave Maria Press, Notre Dame, Indiana 46556, pp. 37-38)

TO THINK AND TALK ABOUT

1. Why did Thomas Merton begin to read the Bible?
2. How did Tom discover that God was missing from his life?
3. How did Tom finally become a writer?

TO READ AND ENJOY:

A Storybook:

SADAKO AND THE THOUSAND PAPER CRANES by Eleanor Coerr (New York: Dell, 1977)

A Poem:

THOMAS MERTON

When we think of
Thomas Merton
We think of
Write and pray.
A Trappist Monk
He did this
As he lived his life
Each day.

When we think of
Thomas Merton
We think of
Books and fame.
A man of God
He wrote well,
Used his gift,
God to proclaim.

Thomas, Merton, Columbia, University, Newspaper, Reporter, Catholic, Church, New, York, United, States, Trappist, Monk, Mahatma, Gandhi, Trappist, Monastery, Gethsemane, Kentucky

JANET MANTERNACH RIPPLE:

A True Story of Triumph over Pain and Death
1934-1982

Janet lived in Carthage, Illinois. Her husband, Richard, is a judge there. They have two children, Jenny and Brett.

Janet was full of life, loved her family and worked hard for their happiness. She was also full of fun. She loved parties. She worked at a local college and had many friends in their small town.

Janet contracted cancer. She fought it for almost ten years. For a while it looked as though she would win out over the attacks of the deadly disease. Then one day the doctors told her the cancer was spreading. She had only a few months to live.

Janet was shocked at the bad news. The next Sunday at Mass her pastor, Father White, noticed how sad Janet looked. He asked her what was wrong and she told him her sad news.

The next morning Father White knocked on Janet's door. "If you have a cup of coffee, I have some donuts to share," he said with a smile. Janet invited him in. They sat down and shared her cof-

fee and his donuts. Most of all they shared her pain and their faith in God.

Janet and Father White had many breakfasts together in the next weeks. Together they struggled to believe that God, who knew Janet's pain, loved her and was with her even in that pain.

Father White suggested that Janet try to pray quietly when she had to lie down to rest. "When I close my eyes, instead of praying," Janet said, "I get afraid of dying and can't rest."

So Father White came one morning with a tape recorder and some cassettes. They contained songs of faith, popular hymns by the St. Louis Jesuits and other musical groups. "When you try to rest, put these songs on quietly. Listen to them and you will be able to relax," Father White suggested.

Janet listened to the songs. She was able to rest. And she was able to deepen her faith. She really did believe that God was with her in her pain, and that God was a caring, good God.

The pain did not go away. In fact it got worse. But her faith and trust in God grew along with the pain. She cried when she thought of leaving her husband and children. She wanted desperately to see Jenny and Brett graduate from high school. Yet she also found peace in the thought that even if she were no longer with them, God would be looking after them.

Her faith in those last months drew people to her. From her pain and faith she was able to help others find strength and hope. She allowed others to help her, and in the process helped them find greater peace in their own troubled lives. She let them love her in her need, and they came to experience a richer love themselves.

One morning just before breakfast Janet died at home with her family. Soon their home was filled with sorrowing friends, neighbors and relatives. Her funeral was a celebration she would have enjoyed. Those who gathered in her home after the funeral felt something of her joy in the midst of their sorrow. All could believe more in God and themselves because of Janet Manternach Ripple.*

*Janet Ripple was Janaan Manternach's sister

JANET MANTERNACH RIPPLE

THE SPIRAL PUZZLE. Begin in the center with No. 1 and fill in the words moving clockwise, spiraling outward. See the clues below.

CLUES:
1. The name of the person the story is about (3 words)
2. The town where she lived
3. The state where she lived
4. Her daughter's name
5. Her son's name
6. The name of the disease that she suffered from
7. The priest who helped her face the disease (2 words)
8. The meals around which Janet and Father White reflected on the mystery of illness and the presence of God
9. A group from St. Louis who composed some of the songs of faith that comforted and helped Janet
10. What grew in her as the disease got worse
11. Besides her children whom did she mind leaving through death?
12. Who she trusted would look after them when she died

TO PRAY AND REMEMBER

HAIL MARY

Hail, Mary, full of grace,
the Lord is with you!

Blessed are you among women,
and blessed is the fruit of your womb, Jesus.

Holy Mary, Mother of God,
pray for us sinners,
now and at the hour of our death.
Amen.

TO THINK AND TALK ABOUT

1. How did Janet's life change after she learned she had only a short time to live?
2. What was Janet's most saving belief?
3. How did Janet affect the lives of others?

TO READ AND ENJOY:

A Storybook:

YOU SHOULDN'T HAVE TO SAY GOODBYE by Patricia Hermes (Harcourt Brace Jovanovich, Publishers, 757 Third Avenue, New York, N.Y. 10017, 1982)

A Poem:

A SISTER

A sister is
Someone you know
And who knows you
As well.

A sister is
Someone to ask
And one also
To tell.

A sister is
Someone who gives
And likes also
To get.

She will not
Just forgive,
She will also
Forget.

I have a sister
And I'll
Always be
Thankful that
She is
A sister
To me.

Key: 1. Janet Manternach Ripple 2. Carthage 3. Illinois 4. Jenny 5. Brett 6. cancer 7. Father White 8. breakfasts 9. Jesuits 10. faith 11. husband 12. God

ST. THOMAS MORE:
A Saintly Statesman
1478-1535

When Thomas More was a young man, he thought about becoming a monk. In fact he lived for several years in a monastery. But he decided God was calling him to marry and to have a family. So he left the monastery.

He studied law at Oxford University and became a lawyer. He married Jane Holt. They had four children. Thomas loved his wife and children. He was a family man. He seemed most to enjoy the time he could spend with them at home.

He and his wife lived in a beautiful home not far from London. They had many friends, and Thomas loved to have them stay with his family.

Thomas More became one of the most important people in all of England. He was one of the most intelligent and best educated men in Europe. Scholars came from many countries to learn from him. He taught his children himself.

A famous student of his was Henry VIII, the King of England. The King was impressed with how intelligent Thomas was. He also came to love him as a friend. He sent Thomas as his personal representative to other countries. He made him a knight. He finally named him to the most important position in the land. He made Thomas More Chancellor of England. Thomas was now second only to the King himself in power.

But then everything changed. King Henry wanted to divorce his wife, Catherine, and marry Anne Boleyn. He wrote to the Pope for permission. The Pope said the King could not divorce Catherine and marry Anne. So King Henry turned against the Pope and named himself head of the Church in England.

Thomas More refused to accept the King as head of the Church. King Henry was very angry. He tried to get Thomas to change his mind. He promised him great rewards. But Thomas would not agree with what the King was doing. He resigned his position as Chancellor.

King Henry tried harder to get Thomas to support him as head of the Church in England. He threatened him and his family. But Thomas would not give in. So the King had Thomas arrested and put in the famous prison, the Tower of London.

During more than a year Thomas' family and friends visited him in prison. They tried to persuade him to change his mind and agree with the King. They reminded him of how happy life would be again at home with those he loved. But Thomas was convinced that what the King wanted was wrong. He refused to accept King Henry as head of the Church.

Finally the King was so angry with Thomas that he had him condemned to death. He accused Thomas of treason, of betraying his country. Thomas was convicted, even though everyone knew he was not a traitor to his country.

Just before Thomas was killed, he turned to the people who were watching. "I die the King's good servant, but God's first," he said. The Church considers Thomas More a saint. We remember him each year on his feast day, June 22.

ST. THOMAS MORE

Find the 17 names and words hidden in the puzzle. They may be vertical, horizontal or diagonal. All the words are in the story.

A	M	O	N	K	L	Z	J	A	N	E	H	O	L	T
N	G	S	A	I	N	T	X	R	Q	Z	E	E	W	C
N	P	D	F	H	C	A	T	H	E	R	I	N	E	K
E	U	R	O	P	E	S	U	P	O	P	E	G	H	M
B	A	Z	Q	L	X	W	T	M	D	R	F	L	Q	O
O	X	F	O	R	D	C	S	D	E	I	J	A	K	N
L	A	B	T	R	E	A	S	O	N	S	L	N	M	A
E	P	O	X	Z	M	R	F	V	W	O	X	D	Y	S
Y	S	B	L	O	N	D	O	N	K	N	I	G	H	T
N	X	C	H	A	N	C	E	L	L	O	R	Z	W	E
A	B	T	C	D	E	F	G	H	I	J	K	L	M	R
K	I	N	G	H	E	N	R	Y	V	I	I	I	R	Y

TO PRAY AND REMEMBER

ACT OF HOPE

My God, I ground my hope completely in you.
You promise
  that all things
    can work together for my good,
  and that absolutely nothing
    can ever separate me from your love.
With you
  good overcomes evil,
  joy transforms sorrow,
  and life conquers death.
Fill me with your Holy Spirit
so I may grow in hope
  no matter what evils I face.
I ask this in the name of Jesus Christ, your Son.
Amen.

(LIVING WATER PRAYERS OF OUR HERITAGE by Carl J. Pfeifer & Janaan Manternach, Paulist Press, p. 49)

TO THINK AND TALK ABOUT

1. What are some qualities of character that you admire in Thomas More?
2. What did Thomas do that was courageous and revealed that he was a person of great integrity?
3. What were Thomas' last words to the people before he was killed?

TO READ AND ENJOY:

A Storybook:

A SUMMER'S WORTH OF SHAME by Colby Rodowsky (Franklin Watts, 730 Fifth Avenue, New York, N.Y. 10019, 1980)

A Poem:

When it is
Hard
To do what's
Right
Do we choose
Wrong
Because of
Fright?
Or do we
Bravely
Hang on
Tight
To what we
Know
Is only
Right?

Key: Anne Boleyn, monk, saint, Jane Holt, Europe, Oxford, Catherine, pope, England, prison, monastery, Thomas More, treason, London, Chancellor, knight, King Henry

MARGARET MEAD:
She Loved Her Work
1901-1978

Margaret slipped into the clear, cold water. The Samoan girls giggled at how white her skin was in the water. Their bodies were a beautiful brown.

"Makelita," they called out to her in the Samoan name they gave her, "let the waves make you jump!"

Margaret relaxed and let the waves lift her up high and then drop her down again. Her Samoan friends laughed with delight. Then they jumped into their favorite swimming hole with her.

Margaret Mead was happy that the young Samoan girls felt so much at home with her. She remembered how shy they were when she first came a few months before. Now they were her friends.

She had traveled halfway around the world to get to know the young girls of Samoa. Margaret was an anthropologist. She came to this distant land to learn how girls grew up in a world so different from her own.

She wanted to know if girls there had the same kinds of problems many American teenage girls have as they grow up. Margaret knew that she could never find out unless she could become as much like a Samoan as possible.

She worked long months learning the Samoan language. She moved to a remote village to live as close to the native people as possible. She spent as much time with the girls and young women as possible during the days. In the evenings, and sometimes long into the night, she made notes on her work.

At times she became very sick. She lived through a terrible hurricane. The tropical heat weakened her. But she worked hard because she believed her work was very important. She believed that what she learned about girls in Samoa might someday be helpful to millions of girls in America.

When she would become tired and discouraged, she remembered something her father told her when she was a young girl: "Adding to the world's store of knowledge is the most important thing a human being can do."

Margaret continued her work in Samoa for almost a year. By then she had discovered what she came to learn. Girls in Samoa did not have the same kinds of problems growing up as American girls do. And Margaret discovered why they did not. It was because they did not have to face the same kinds of pressures to succeed and be popular that American girls feel.

She came back home and worked hard for months writing a book from the notes she wrote in Samoa. She called her book, *Coming Of Age In Samoa.* It was a very popular, helpful book.

Margaret Mead then went to other distant parts of the world to learn more about people and the way they live. She became very famous because of her work. She loved her work so much that she did not retire. She worked up to a few weeks before she died at the age of 76.

She worked hard because she shared her father's belief that "adding to the world's store of knowledge is the most important thing a human being can do."

1.	2.
3.	4.
5.	6.
7.	8.
9.	10.
11.	12.
13.	14.
15.	16.
17.	18.
19.	20.

MARGARET MEAD

TWO WORD PUZZLE. When the grid below is completed each pair of adjacent boxes will contain a two word answer. Clues are identified by the numbers in the boxes that correspond with the phrases below.

CLUES:
1- 2 The name of a great anthropologist
3- 4 The color of the Samoan girls' skin
5- 6 "Makelita"
7- 8 Distance Margaret traveled around the world to get to Samoa
9-10 The age of the girls that Margaret was interested in
11-12 The language Margaret learned
13-14 The kind of climate Margaret suffered from in Samoa
15-16 Another way to refer to people
17-18 A place where Margaret moved to be as close as she could to the native people
19-20 The age Margaret was when she died

TO PRAY AND REMEMBER

ACT OF THANKSGIVING

My God and Father,
I thank you for everything:

for the fascinating world about me,
for people near and far,
for myself,
so filled with wondrous powers.
All that is,
is your gift.
All that I am and have
I receive from you.
I thank you for everything,
through Jesus Christ, your Son,
in whom you give us
all good things.

(LIVING WATER PRAYERS OF OUR HERITAGE by Carl J. Pfeifer & Janaan Manternach, Paulist Press, pp. 62-63)

TO THINK AND TALK ABOUT

1. What did Margaret Mead have to do in Samoa so that she could gain the information she wanted?
2. What kept Margaret going through hard and discouraging times?
3. How do you feel about the belief that Margaret shared with her father?

TO READ AND ENJOY:

A Storybook:

ONE SMALL BLUE BEAD by Byrd Baylor Schweitzer (Macmillan Publishing Company, Inc., 866 Third Avenue, New York, N.Y. 10022, 1965)

A Poem:

MARGARET MEAD

To learn an
Unknown,
To probe
Mystery
Can add to the
Story of
Humanity.
Margaret Mead
Lived
Her Life
Adding to knowledge's
Store.
And because of her
We know
Of life
More.

Margaret, Mead, beautiful, brown, Samoan, name, half, way, teen, age, Samoan, language, tropical, heat, human, being, remote, village, seventy, six

43

TEILHARD de CHARDIN:
Finding The Future in the Past
1881-1955

Pierre loved to take walks through the woods with his father. Their home was in a rugged part of France with many hills and dark woods.

He was amazed at how his father knew the names of all the trees and flowers, the rocks and minerals. Pierre and his father picked up many interesting objects during these walks. They added them to their collections at home.

Pierre's mother was excited each time the two came in from their walks. She greeted them with tea and cookies. Pierre showed her each rock and flower they picked up. He carefully added each one to the growing collections.

Pierre's greatest find was a piece of iron from an old plow. He kept it in a secret place. He loved to take it out and rub his hands over it. He liked it because it felt so solid and strong. But then he discovered that it could rust. That made him sad.

He then became fascinated with some of the colored stones he found in the area around their house. He loved quartz crystals. They were solid but let light through.

His childhood love for iron and rocks and everything close to the earth remained with Pierre Teilhard de Chardin all during his life. When he was a young Jesuit studying in England he never took a walk without taking along a magnifying glass and a small hammer. With the hammer he broke open rocks he found. Then he could look at them carefully with the magnifying glass. He was learning to be a scientist.

He marveled at the solidness of things. He felt close to the world and everything in it. Pierre seemed to find God everywhere in the world. He felt that the Spirit of Christ was alive in the world drawing the world to become more hospitable for people. As he grew older he learned to find Christ also in people.

He became a priest, but continued his work as a scientist. He went to Egypt to study and teach. There he discovered the remains of a world long past—pyramids and tombs, the Nile River, the desert. His contact with the past sparked his interest in the future.

Then he went to China. There he discovered the bones of a pre-historic man. It was an important scientific discovery. Pierre sensed that the Spirit of Christ was drawing people over the centuries to a better life, a more loving life.

Pierre Teilhard de Chardin spent his last years in New York. People who knew him were impressed by his scientific knowledge. He still loved to look at rocks and flowers as he walked in Central Park. He still studied relics of ancient times.

But people who knew him were even more impressed by his love of people and of God. He seemed to find God everywhere, but most of all in people. He was kind and sensitive. He listened to others as few people listened. He suffered much, but was mostly cheerful and full of hope. Many people consider him a saint.

TEILHARD de CHARDIN

MEANING OR MATCHING. Find in the story words that match or mean the same thing as the clue word.

1.	forest	(woods)
2.	plants	(flowers)
3.	metal	(iron)
4.	land	(earth)
5.	Big Apple	(New York)
6.	crystals	(quartz)
7.	Jesuit	(priest)
8.	magnifying	(glass)
9.	tea	(cookies)
10.	Nile	(River)

TO PRAY AND REMEMBER

ACT OF LOVE

My God, I love you
  because you are so good,
    and because you love me so much.
I love you
  in loving myself,
    because your love makes me lovable.
I love you
  in loving other people,
    because your love gives them life and dignity.
I love you
  in loving the world,
    because the world reveals your creative presence.
Through your Holy Spirit
  let my love grow ever deeper,
I ask this in Jesus' name. Amen.

(LIVING WATER PRAYERS OF OUR HERITAGE by Pfeifer/Manternach, Paulist Press, pp.56-57)

TO THINK AND TALK ABOUT

1. What was a childhood love of Pierre Teilhard de Chardin that remained with him all through his life?
2. What are some things that Pierre sensed about the world?
3. What were Pierre's greatest loves?

TO READ AND ENJOY:

A Storybook:

EVERYBODY NEEDS A ROCK by Byrd Baylor (New York: Scribner's Sons, 1974)

A Poem:

PIERRE TEILHARD de CHARDIN

In nature God is present
In ways forever new.
Pierre Chardin discovered this
Is true of people, too.

A Jesuit and a scientist
Most sensitive and kind
Suffered but was full of hope.
In him a saint we'll find.

TITUS BRANDSMA:
A Strong But Gentle Priest
1881-1942

It was evening. The sun was setting slowly over the monastery in Holland.

Father Titus heard a loud banging on the monastery door. He went to open it. He felt a tremor of fear as he opened the heavy door. Three Nazi Gestapo officers stood there with guns.

"We have orders to arrest Fr. Titus Brandsma," the chief officer said coldly.

"I am Fr. Titus," the priest answered. The officers allowed him to say goodbye to his superior. The superior blessed him, and Fr. Titus left the monastery under heavy guard.

"Imagine my going to jail at the age of 60," he said with a smile to the arresting officer.

"You should not have spoken out against us," the man answered without a smile.

"As a Catholic, I could have done nothing differently," Titus answered.

"You are a saboteur, an enemy," the officer charged.

They took Fr. Titus to prison and locked him in a cell.

The scholarly Carmelite priest spent his time in prayer and study. He started writing a book. "I pray, I write . . . I am very calm. I am happy," he wrote in a letter to his superior.

But then he was moved to a worse prison. He and the other prisoners were forced to work all day chopping down trees. They had little to eat. Many became sick and died. Others were shot.

Prisoners who were released told their friends about Fr. Titus. "He often gave some of his little food to other starving prisoners," one remembered. "I was touched by his special care for the Jews," confessed another.

Fr. Titus quietly encouraged his fellow prisoners. He secretly heard their confessions and led them in prayer. He asked them to forgive those who were beating and starving them.

Finally the Gestapo decided to punish Fr. Titus even more severely. "We have decided to move you to Dachau," the Captain told him. "You will stay there until the end of the war."

Dachau was a concentration camp. Few who went there ever came back. Hundreds of thousands were put to death at Dachau.

At Dachau the guards were vicious. They frequently beat Fr. Titus with clubs. His quiet courage angered them. They kicked him and beat him until he was nearly unconscious.

The guards forced the prisoners to work hard from 5:30 in the morning until 7:00 in the evening. There was less food than in the other prisons. The prisoners became weak and sick.

Fr. Titus also became very sick. But he continued to think of others. He shared whatever he had with his fellow prisoners. He continued to encourage his prisoners not to lose faith. "Do not give in to hatred," he whispered to them.

Finally he was taken to the hospital to be part of a cruel experiment. A doctor injected him with a powerful drug. Ten minutes later Fr. Titus Brandsma, who brought life and love to so many, was dead.

TITUS BRANDSMA

Unscramble the words below. All the words are in the story.

EILMACTER

AUDHCA

TTISU

RRSPINOES

DBNMSARA

DLLHANO

NNNCTAROECIOC

SSNOICFENOS

AGSTPOE

CCOLTIAH

YESTNMARO

TPREIS

TO PRAY AND REMEMBER

ACT OF HOPE

My God, I ground my hope completely in you.
You promise
  that all things
    can work together for my good,
  and that absolutely nothing
    can ever separate me from your love.
With you
  good overcomes evil,
  joy transforms sorrow,
  and life conquers death.
Fill me with your Holy Spirit
  so I may grow in hope
    no matter what evils I face.
I ask this in the name of Jesus Christ,
  your Son.
Amen.

(LIVING WATER PRAYERS OF OUR HERITAGE by C. Pfeifer & J. Manternach, Paulist Press, p.49)

TO THINK AND TALK ABOUT

1. How and why was Father Titus arrested and imprisoned?

2. How did Father Titus spend his time in the first two prisons that he was in?
3. How was Father Titus treated at Dachau and what did he urge his fellow prisoners not to do?

TO READ AND ENJOY:

A Storybook:

TWENTY AND TEN by Claire Huchet Bishop (Penguin Books, 625 Madison Avenue, New York, N.Y. 10022, 1952)

A Poem:

TITUS BRANDSMA

A cell may hold your body
But your spirit remains free
To love and hope and struggle,
To be who you can be.

Titus Brandsma was arrested
And a prisoner became,
A sign of truth to others
That they were not to blame.

(Carmelite, Dachau, Titus, prisoners, Brandsma, Holland, concentration, priest, monastery, Catholic, Gestapo, confessions)

47

ST. THERESE OF LISIEUX:
A Loving Woman
1873-1897

Therese Martin was born into a large family. She was the youngest of nine children. Naturally she was the family favorite.

Her father was a watch-maker and her mother made lace. They had worked hard and were very well off. They loved each other and their children very much. When Therese was just four years old her mother died.

Therese was a very pretty young girl. She was also very bright and full of life. She could also be stubborn at times.

Therese grew up surrounded by the love of her parents and her four brothers and four sisters. She enjoyed family games. She especially loved to go fishing with her father.

She felt loved from the very beginning. As she grew, she felt just as sure of God's love for her.

She learned at home to trust and love God. She also learned to care about others by watching how her parents and older brothers and sisters loved one another. She saw, too, how generous they were to anyone in need.

One after another each of her older sisters became Carmelite nuns. By the time she was a teenager she was eager to join the Carmelites herself. She felt it would be her way of loving God and other people the best way she possibly could.

Since she was still so young, the bishop of Lisieux, where her family lived, would not let Therese become a nun. She went with her family to Rome, and met Pope Leo XIII. She boldly asked him to let her become a Carmelite even though she was just fifteen. He did not refuse, so she entered the Carmelite convent.

She spent her life as a nun in that same convent in Lisieux. Few people ever heard of her. She followed the same routine of prayer, work and recreation that the other nuns followed. But she did so with great love for God and others.

Her heart seemed to take in the whole world and everyone's problems. Even though her life was spent within the walls of the convent, she prayed for people everywhere. She prayed especially for missionaries who were working to help people all over the world come to know and love Jesus Christ.

She wished that she could give her life for Christ, as so many martyrs did. But she found she could love God and others in more ordinary ways. She tried to be kind to the sisters she lived with. She tried to be patient and understanding when they did things that bothered her. She helped them in many small ways.

Her superiors were so impressed with Sister Therese's prayerful and caring life that they asked her to write her autobiography. In it she told the secret of her life. She wrote that she trusted completely in God's love for her. And she tried to love God and her sisters by doing the ordinary things of her daily life as well as possible. She called it her "little way."

Therese's "little way" became known when her autobiography was published after her early death at age 23. All over the world people read about Therese and tried to live her "little way" of love and trust. The Church calls her a saint and honors her every year on her feast day, October 1.

TO PRAY AND REMEMBER

PRAYER OF OUR LOVE
FOR GOD ALONE

My God,
you know that I have always desired
to love you alone.
I seek no other glory.
Your love has preceded me
from the time of my childhood,
become greater with my youth,
and is presently an abyss
whose depth I cannot fathom.
  St. Therese of Lisieux (1873-1897)

(NEW SAINT JOSEPH'S PEOPLE'S PRAYER BOOK, #540,
p. 430)

TO THINK AND TALK ABOUT

1. How is your life as a child different/the same as
   Therese Martin's?
2. What are some important things that Therese
   learned in her family?
3. How did Therese become a saint?

TO READ AND ENJOY:

A Storybook:

BROOKIE AND HER LAMB by M. B. Goffstein
(Farrar, Straus & Giroux, Inc., 19 Union Square W.,
New York, N.Y. 10003, 1979)

A Poem:

THERESE OF LISIEUX

Therese lived well a "little way"
And she's remembered to this day.

ST. THERESE OF LISIEUX

Using the clues below, work the crossword puzzle.

DOWN:
  2. The name of the religious order that Therese joined
  3. This is what the story of one's life is called
  5. This is what Therese was when she wanted to join the
     Carmelites
  6. This is the kind of work Therese's father did
  7. This is something that she especially loved to do with
     her father
  8. This is what Therese called her life as a nun
  10. The city where Therese lived
  12. This is what the Church calls Therese of Lisieux

ACROSS:
  1. This is what Therese told of her life in her autobiogra-
     phy
  4. This is the age Therese was when her mother died
  9. The person that she learned to love and trust at home
  11. The first and last name of the person the story is
     about
  13. The age Therese was when she entered the convent

Secret, Four, Therese Martin, Fifteen, Carmelites,
Autobiography, Teenager, Watch Maker, Fishing, Little Way,
Lisieux, Saint

Jew and observed the traditional Jewish customs.

Edith was the youngest child. She was full of life and loved to play hide-and-seek with her brothers and sisters. She was very bright.

She loved to study and learn. She was always near the top of her class in school.

As she grew older, Edith had many questions about life. She began a lifelong search for the meaning of life.

The more she learned the less she believed in God. She observed Jewish practices only to please her mother. She no longer felt that religion had anything important to say about life.

Edith went on to the university. She studied philosophy, always trying to get below the surface of things. She loved to study and read. It was very unusual for a woman at that time to study philosophy. Edith strongly believed in women's rights. She gave many talks about the importance of women in the world.

One day she went to the funeral of an old friend. She was amazed at the courage of the man's widow. Edith asked her where she found the strength to cope with her husband's death. The widow was a Christian and told her about Christ. She said that she believed her husband was with God.

This experience changed the course of Edith's life. She began to pray. She read the life of St. Teresa of Avila. She learned more about Christianity. After several years, Edith decided to become a Catholic.

Her mother cried when Edith told her. She felt that Edith was rejecting everything she and her family believed in and taught her. Edith's mother was even more upset when Edith decided to become a Carmelite Sister.

Edith was very happy as a sister. She continued to read and study. She prayed for hours. She loved the quiet. She wrote books on the meaning of life and the importance of faith.

Then war came to Germany. Edith had to leave Germany because she was a Jew. She went to the Carmelite convent in Holland.

Germany soon invaded Holland. The Nazis searched out all Jews there, too. They soon discovered Edith, and her sister, Rosa, who was there with her.

They were arrested and placed in a prison camp. It was a terrible place. People suffered terribly. Edith did, too. But she did all she could to help others. She shared everything with others. "Whatever may happen to Rosa and me, we are ready," she told some friends. "Christ is with us even here."

Not long afterward Edith Stein and her sister were put to death. She prayed and helped others right up to the end. She had found in Christ's cross the real meaning of life.

EDITH STEIN:
A Wise Woman
1891-1942

From the day she was born Edith was a remarkable girl. Her father loved her dearly. So did her mother. Unfortunately Edith's father died when Edith was just two years old.

Edith's mother was a strong and good woman. She raised her children and also took over her husband's lumber company. She was a devout

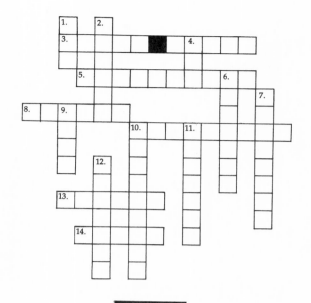

EDITH STEIN

Using the clues below, work the crossword puzzle.

DOWN:
1. What Edith was that brought about her death
2. She believed so much in these for women that she gave many talks to promote them
4. Edith's age when her father died
6. The country where she lived as a Carmelite
7. The religious tradition Edith chose
9. Her sister's name
10. The religion of the widow who influenced the course of Edith's life
11. In life she searched for this
12. The country Edith had to leave because she was a Jew

ACROSS:
3. The name of the woman that the story is about (2 words)
5. The subject Edith studied at the university
10. The kind of Sister that she became
13. The first name of a great saint whose life Edith read
14. The German soldiers who arrested Edith and her sister

TO PRAY AND REMEMBER

THE APOSTLES' CREED

I believe in God,
  the Father almighty,
  Creator of heaven and earth;
And in Jesus Christ,
  his only Son,
  our Lord,
    who was conceived by the Holy Spirit,
    born of the Virgin Mary,

suffered under Pontius Pilate,
  was crucified,
  died, and was buried.
  He descended into hell;
  the third day he arose again from the dead;
  he ascended into heaven,
  sitteth at the right hand of God,
  the Father almighty,
  from thence he shall come
  to judge the living and the dead.
I believe in the Holy Spirit,
  the Holy Catholic Church,
  the communion of saints,
  the forgiveness of sins,
  the resurrection of the body,
  and life everlasting.
Amen.

(LIVING WATER PRAYERS OF OUR HERITAGE by C. Pfeifer & J. Manternach, Paulist Press, p. 23)

TO THINK AND TALK ABOUT

1. How is your childhood different from and how is it similar to Edith Stein's?
2. What led up to Edith's decision to become a Carmelite Sister?
3. Why and how did Edith die?

TO READ AND ENJOY:

A Storybook:

LISTEN FOR THE SINGING by Jean Little (E. P. Dutton, 201 Park Avenue South, New York, N.Y. 10003, 1977)

A Poem:

EDITH STEIN

People who are prejudiced
Often fail to see
That people who are not like them
Are as good or better be.

People who are prejudiced
Down through history
Have caused a lot of suffering
Because of bigotry.

Edith Stein was hunted
Because she was a Jew,
Taken to a prison camp
And put to death there, too.

Jew, Rights, Two, Holland, Catholic, Rosa, Christian, Meaning, Germany, Edith Stein, Philosophy, Christ, Carmelite, Teresa, Nazis

ST. THOMAS AQUINAS:
A Great Thinker
1225-1274

Thomas was born in a castle. He was the youngest son of a soldier and his wife. He had five sisters and three brothers.

Because his country was at war so much, Thomas' father was away most of the time. His mother and older brothers and sisters raised him.

When he was five years old, his mother sent him to school at the famous Benedictine abbey, Monte Cassino. She hoped that he would stay there and become a Benedictine monk. Secretly she dreamed that he would become the abbot or superior. As abbot, he would be famous, powerful and rich.

Thomas studied hard. He liked to learn. He had a tremendous curiosity about everything. He kept asking his teachers "Why this?" and "Why that?" The question he wondered most about was about God. "What is God?" he asked his teachers.

He kept asking that question as a teenager at the University in Naples. His teachers gave him some answers. But Thomas knew that there had to be more to know about God. He really wanted to know God more than anyone or anything else.

One of his teachers gave him the books of a very ancient Greek philosopher named Aristotle. Nothing excited Thomas as much as these books. From Aristotle he learned to look at everything in a new way. He believed that Aristotle's ideas would help him better understand the mysteries of life. He also felt that they would help him learn more about God.

Thomas became the friend of one of his teachers. The teacher was a member of a new religious group called Dominicans. The Dominicans were teachers and preachers. Their whole work was to learn about God and to teach others about God.

Thomas decided to become a Dominican. It meant that he would never reach his mother's dream. He would never be a powerful abbot of a rich monastery. Dominicans were poor. His mother was so upset that she had Thomas' oldest brother capture him and bring him back home.

But Thomas was determined to be a Dominican. Finally his mother let him go. He went to Cologne and became a Dominican. He continued to study about life and about God.

Thomas was very big. He stood six foot six. He was also a quiet young man. His classmates called him the "Dumb Ox." Thomas just smiled and went on studying.

Soon he became a teacher. He began to write about his ideas of life and God. He became very famous all over Europe. He was one of the smartest men of his time. But he never stopped searching for more knowledge of God and the world.

His ideas were new and exciting. He used the works of Aristotle to explain what God was like. This made many important people very angry. They were afraid of Thomas' new ideas. They made life very difficult for Thomas.

But Thomas continued his search to understand life and God until he died. The Church calls Thomas Aquinas a saint and the patron of students. We honor St. Thomas Aquinas each January 28.

ST. THOMAS AQUINAS

Find the ten words hidden in the puzzle. They may be vertical, horizontal or diagonal. All the words are in the story.

P	T	E	A	C	H	E	R	S	D
R	E	Q	R	S	T	U	A	V	O
E	U	L	M	G	C	M	O	P	M
A	R	I	S	T	O	T	L	E	I
C	O	F	G	H	L	D	J	K	N
H	P	X	T	Z	O	R	D	B	I
E	E	M	P	R	G	K	U	Z	C
R	A	Q	U	I	N	A	S	Q	A
S	O	K	L	M	E	D	H	W	N
X	S	T	U	D	E	N	T	S	R

TO PRAY AND REMEMBER

FOR THE NEEDY

Grant, Lord, that I may gladly share
what I have with the needy,
humbly ask for what I need from him who has,
sincerely admit the evil I have done,
calmly bear the evil I suffer,
not envy my neighbor for his blessings,
and thank you unceasingly
whenever you hear my prayer.
St. Thomas Aquinas (1225-1274)

(LORD, HEAR OUR PRAYER compiled by Thomas McNally, C.S.C., Ave Maria Press, Notre Dame Indiana 46556, 1978, p. 49)

TO THINK AND TALK ABOUT

1. Why did Thomas Aquinas study hard?
2. What was the question that he wondered about most?
3. How did Thomas react to the name his classmates gave him?
4. Why do you feel that St. Thomas is the patron of students?

TO READ AND ENJOY:

A Storybook:

YUSSEL'S PRAYER by Barbara Cohen (Lothrop, Lee & Shepard Company, 105 Madison Ave., New York, N.Y. 10016, 1981)

A Poem:

WHO IS GOD?

"Who is God?"
The child asked.
"I wonder,
God is who?"

"You are the answer"
Said her Mom,
"And I'm the
Answer, too.

And all you see
Of plant and tree
The stars and moon
And sun.

The answer
To your question, child,
Is still a bigger
One."

Key: teacher, preachers, Europe, students, Cologne, God, Aristotle, Thomas, Dominican, Aquinas

53

ELIZABETH ANN SETON:
A Great Mother, A Great Nun
1774-1821

Elizabeth was a charming girl. She had brown eyes and milk white skin. She was bright and beautiful.

But she knew pain and sorrow very early. Her mother died when she was just three. It was just the first of many great sorrows.

She loved her father very much. He was a doctor. She liked to watch for him through the window and then run out to give him a big hug and kiss.

As she grew to be a young women, Elizabeth became still more beautiful. She learned to ride horses and play musical instruments. She was very popular. Everyone liked her.

Then she met William. He fell in love with her and she with him. They married and settled down in New York. William was a successful businessman. Elizabeth and William were very happy. Their five children added to their joy.

But pain and sorrow soon changed Elizabeth's life. William's business failed. They lost everything.

Then her father died of yellow fever. Elizabeth was very sad. Her pain led her to read the Bible and to pray to God for strength.

William became very ill. Elizabeth had to sell the last of her possessions to care for him. But he died. She was now all alone with her children to raise. Only her faith in God helped her go on. Elizabeth decided to become a Catholic.

She worked hard to support herself and her children. Some friends let her stay in the upstairs rooms of their house. She was poor, but she trusted even more in God.

A priest invited her to Baltimore to teach children. He provided a place for her and her children to live. After a while the Bishop of Baltimore invited Elizabeth to go to Emmitsburg, Maryland. Besides her three daughters she took with her four young women who wanted to live and work with her. Elizabeth and the four women called themselves "Sisters of Charity." People called Elizabeth, "Mother Seton."

At Emmitsburg Elizabeth and her sisters started a school for girls. Rich parents paid to have their daughters in Mother Seton's school. Poor children were allowed into the school free. Elizabeth was happy working hard for people and for God.

But sorrow and death were never far away. Two of her daughters died during the next few years.

So did her two sisters-in-law. Elizabeth's heart was full of sorrow, but also full of trust in God.

People loved Mother Seton. She was always reaching out to others. She started more schools. More and more young women were attracted to her and her work. Her community of "Sisters of Charity" kept growing.

Each new problem brought its pain and sorrow to Mother Seton, but she trusted more and more in God. She seemed to grow stronger as the years went on, discovering strength she never suspected she had. But then, far from being old, she became very sick and died on January 4, 1821. Today the Church honors her as Saint Elizabeth Seton, and celebrates her feast on that day.

ELIZABETH ANN SETON

Unscramble the words below. All the words are in the story.

R E M O B L T A I

Y R A A J U N

L L M I A W I

G M M E I S G R U B

T I C R A H Y

T B L A E I Z E H

O C A C H L T I

I L B E B D

M L N Y R A A

N E T S O

TO PRAY AND REMEMBER

GLORY BE

Glory be to the Father,
  and to the Son,
  and to the Holy Spirit.
as it was in the beginning, is now
  and ever shall be world without end.
Amen.

(LIVING WATER PRAYERS OF OUR HERITAGE by C. Pfeifer & J. Manternach, Paulist Press, p. 26)

TO THINK AND TALK ABOUT

1. What brought a lot of sorrow into Elizabeth's life?
2. What was Elizabeth's life like after her husband died?
3. Why do you feel that the Church honors Elizabeth Seton as a saint?

TO READ AND ENJOY:

A Storybook:

TREAD SOFTLY by Corrine Gerson (The Dial Press, 1 Dag Hammarskjold Plaza, New York, N.Y. 10017, 1979)

A Poem:

ELIZABETH SETON

No matter what happens,
No matter how bad,
We have it within us
To trust and be glad.

Elizabeth Seton had
Troubles galore
But no matter how heavy
Her trouble she bore.

She started a school
For pay and for free
And began an Order
Sisters of Charity.

(Baltimore, January, William, Emmitsburg, charity, Elizabeth, Catholic, bible, Maryland, Seton)

55

FATHER FLANAGAN OF BOYS TOWN:

A Respecter of Youth 1886-1948

Father Flanagan sat at his desk thinking. "These figures are amazing," he said to himself. He was reviewing his studies of 2,000 homeless, hopeless men. They had passed through his Workingman's Hotel in Omaha, Nebraska.

"Nine out of ten of these men grew up in broken homes," he read to himself from his notes. "I wonder if they would be living on the streets today, if they had grown up in homes where there was respect and love," he thought to himself.

There was a knock at his door. He opened it. He looked down at a small boy carrying a canvas bag full of newspapers.

"Can I stay here?" the boy asked.

"Of course," Father Flanagan responded. "At least for a few days. This is a hotel for older people than newsboys."

Within a few weeks there were five newspaper boys staying there. They had no homes. They had been living on the streets.

Father Flanagan realized that the down-and-out men who came to his hotel had once been like these boys. He made a tough decision.

"I can't run two hotels, one for the men and another for the boys. There just isn't enough money or time. It is more important to help these youngsters. They can still be helped to live better lives."

So Father Flanagan closed the Workingman's Hotel and found a house for himself and the newsboys. Soon he had twenty boys. He came to love them and to believe in them. They grew in love for themselves and for Father Flanagan.

But few people believed in Fr. Flanagan and his home for boys. No one would help him. He had no more money. So he turned to publicity to draw attention and contributions to his boys.

"There's no such thing as a bad boy," he kept saying. Gradually the message got across. Famous actors, athletes, and movie stars came to visit Father Flanagan's home for boys. Soon he and his boys were famous.

More and more boys came to his home. Parents brought their boys to Father Flanagan. Judges sent boys who were in trouble to the home in Omaha. He now had 200 boys to care for.

Father Flanagan bought a farm outside the city and named it Boys' Town. He believed that youngsters were basically good. He respected them and trusted them to grow. He asked them to help run Boys' Town. He gave them freedom and responsibility.

Boys' Town and Father Flanagan became even more famous. A movie about him and his boys was made. The President of the United States asked Father Flanagan's advice and help in dealing with young people.

Father Flanagan is dead. But Boys' Town still exists. Hundreds of boys continue to find hope and a home there. Father Flanagan's spirit can be sensed from a statue that stands at Boys' Town. A boy is carrying a younger boy. The older boy is saying, "No, he's not heavy. He's my brother."

FATHER FLANAGAN OF BOYS TOWN

MEANING OR MATCHING. Find in the story words that match or mean the same things as the clue word.

1. Workingman's	(Hotel)
2. news	(boys or paper)
3. Boys	(town)
4. broken	(homes)
5. canvas	(bag)
6. Father	(Flanagan)
7. movie	(stars)
8. United	(States)
9. contributions	(money)
10. monument	(statue)
11. Omaha	(Nebraska)
12. figures	(numbers)

TO PRAY AND REMEMBER

ST. PATRICK'S BREASTPLATE

Christ to shield me today...
Christ with me, Christ before me, Christ behind me,
Christ in me, Christ beneath me, Christ above me,
Christ on my right, Christ on my left,
Christ when I lie down, Christ when I sit down,
Christ when I arise,
Christ in the heart of every man who thinks of me,
Christ in the mouth of everyone who speaks of me,
Christ in every eye that sees me,
Christ in every ear that hears me.

(LIVING WATER PRAYERS OF OUR HERITAGE by C. Pfeifer & J. Manternach, Paulist Press, p. 98)

TO THINK AND TALK ABOUT

1. Why did Father Flanagan decide to run a home for boys rather than for homeless men?
2. How did Father Flanagan's dream grow?
3. How successful was Father Flanagan's home for boys and what is the spirit that still inspires the place?

TO READ AND ENJOY:

A Storybook:

I BE SOMEBODY by Irwin Hadley (Atheneum Publishers, 122 E. 42 St., New York, N.Y. 10017, 1984)

A Poem:

CHOOSE THE LOVING THING

We cannot know
If someone's
Bad
Or someone's very
Good.
But we believe
That everyone
Collects a lot of
"Shoulds."
And most,
If given half a
Chance,
And maybe even
Two,
Will choose what is
The loving
Thing
And that is
What they'll
Do.

ST. MARGARET OF SCOTLAND:
A Dedicated Family
1045-1093

Margaret was a beautiful young princess. She was related to three Kings of England.

But her beauty and her royalty were no protection in time of war. The armies of William the Conqueror invaded England. Margaret and her brother escaped from England in a ship.

A terrible storm wrecked the ship off the coast of Scotland. Margaret and her brother survived the shipwreck. King Malcolm of Scotland took them into his palace.

The King immediately fell in love with the beautiful young princess. He begged Margaret to marry him and become his Queen. Margaret hesitated for a while. The King was a rough man who could neither read nor write. He had a bad temper and poor manners. But Margaret sensed that Malcolm was a good man. She came to love him and became his wife and queen.

Margaret and Malcolm had a large family. They loved their six sons and two daughters very much. Margaret took charge of the children's education. She and Malcolm were concerned that their children would share their Christian faith and their sense of responsibility as leaders of the Scottish people. Three of the boys later became Kings of Scotland. The people of Scotland believed the youngest, King David, was a saint.

The children grew up seeing their parents living out the ideals they taught them. Margaret and Malcolm loved each other very much. Margaret's love gradually changed the King into a more gentle, caring man.

The King and Queen prayed together each day.

They worked hard together to govern Scotland well. They tried to make life better for everyone in their country. They supported the Church by their own example of prayer and compassion as well as by generous gifts of money.

People were most impressed by how the King and Queen personally cared for the poor. Whenever the Queen rode out into the countryside, poor people flocked around her. She gave them money and clothes. She and her husband paid the ransom of hundreds of slaves so they could be free women and men. The two of them built shelters for pilgrims to Scotland's shrines.

Each morning, before she and the King had breakfast, Queen Margaret fed nine orphans. Then she and Malcolm served food to 300 poor people who came to the palace. They then prayed together in the church for a while, and Margaret waited on twenty-four poor people whom she supported until she died. Only then did the King and Queen themselves eat breakfast.

The people of Scotland were very sad when their good and beautiful Queen became very ill. For four years she suffered. Malcolm took good care of her.

Then one day an enemy army attacked Scotland. King Malcolm was killed. Margaret was very sad. Four days later she died. She and Malcolm had been married for twenty-three years. They were two of Scotland's greatest rulers. The Church honors Margaret as the patroness of Scotland. Her feastday is March 9.

1.	2.
3.	4.
5.	6.
7.	8.
9.	10.
11.	12.
13.	14.
15.	16.
17.	18.
19.	20.

ST. MARGARET OF SCOTLAND

TWO WORD PUZZLE. When the grid below is completed each pair of adjacent boxes will contain a two word answer. Clues are identified by the numbers in the boxes that correspond with the phrases below.

CLUES:
1- 2 Special people in England who were relatives of Margaret
3- 4 A tragedy that Margaret and her brother survived
5- 6 The man Margaret married
7- 8 The number of Margaret and Malcolm's children
9-10 The people Margaret and her family were responsible for
11-12 The son that the people of Scotland thought was a saint
13-14 Margaret's name after she married Malcolm
15-16 The number of poor people that Margaret and Malcolm supported until they died
17-18 The number of years Margaret and Malcolm were married
19-20 This is what the two of them were to the people of Scotland

TO PRAY AND REMEMBER

You shall love the Lord your God
with all your heart,
with all your soul,
with all your strength,
and with all your mind;
and your neighbor as yourself.
Luke 10:27

TO THINK AND TALK ABOUT

1. What caused Margaret to hesitate to become Malcolm's wife and why did she change her mind?
2. What was life like for Margaret after she married Malcolm?
3. Why are Margaret and Malcolm considered two of Scotland's greatest rulers?

TO READ AND ENJOY:

A Storybook:

SIDEWALK STORY by Sharon Bell Mathis (The Viking Press, 625 Madison Avenue, New York, N.Y. 10022, 1971)

A Poem:

MARGARET AND MALCOLM OF SCOTLAND

A king and queen
Of Scotland,
Margaret, Malcolm
Were their names.
They ruled with
Love and gentleness
And for caring
Were acclaimed.
They fed the poor
And hungry,
Cared for orphans,
Slaves they freed.
They spent their years
As King and Queen
Helping those in need.

three, kings, ship, wreck, King, Malcolm, eight, children, Scottish, people, King, David, Queen, Margaret, twenty, four, twenty, three, greatest, rulers

ALBERT SCHWEITZER:
A Man of Reverence
1875-1965

Albert was just eight or nine years old. He was riding a gentle, old horse a farmer let him ride. Suddenly a big dog ran barking toward the horse. The horse reared up in fear.

Albert lashed out at the dog with a long whip. The whip stung the dog in the left eye. The dog fell to the ground and rolled over and over yelping in pain.

Albert had not meant to hurt the dog, just to scare it away. For weeks he could not get the sight of the injured dog out of his mind. He made up a prayer which he prayed the rest of his life, "Heavenly Father, protect and bless all living creatures."

As he grew older, Albert became more sensitive to pain. It hurt him to see animals suffering. It hurt him even more to see suffering people.

Albert loved music. He learned to play the piano and the organ, and he gave concerts. And Albert, the son of a Lutheran pastor, also became a theologian and wrote a book about Jesus. He became a famous man and had everything a young man could want.

But he thought often of those who had so much less, people who were poor and sick, people with no money or education. He could feel their pain and wanted to do something about it.

He decided to give up his music and his teaching and his security. He and his wife decided to go to the jungles of Africa to help the very poor. He became a doctor and his wife became a nurse.

They went to Africa and set up a little hospital in the jungle. Sick people came from everywhere. Albert and his wife worked almost day and night to ease people's pain. People were suffering not just from diseases, but from injuries caused by enemies. The jungle was a frightening place. So was the world which was in the middle of the First World War.

"Why is it that people hurt each other so much?" Dr. Schweitzer asked himself. "Why is there so much fighting? Why are there wars? What is needed to make the world better?"

One evening he discovered his answer. He was riding on a barge up a wide river. It was still hot as the sun dropped behind the hills. A herd of huge hippopotamuses moved slowly in the waters around the barge. Suddenly a thought flashed through his mind, "Reverence for Life."

That was his answer to what the world needed most. If people had a reverence for life, for all liv-

ing things, they would not keep hurting one another. There would be no wars.

Reverence for life is what he had felt when he hurt the dog that frightened his horse as a young boy. Reverence for life was what he felt when he rescued an orphaned baby monkey in the jungle. Reverence for life was what brought him and his wife to the jungles to ease people's pain.

After 52 years of caring for the sick in the African jungle, Albert Schweitzer summed up his deepest conviction: "If a man loses reverence for any part of life, he will lose his reverence for all life."

ALBERT SCHWEITZER

THE SPIRAL PUZZLE. Begin in the center with No. 1 and fill in the words moving clockwise, spiraling outward. See the clues below.

CLUES:
1. The name of the person the story is about (2 words)
2. The animal he hurt when he was a child
3. & 4. The creatures that it hurt him to see suffer
5. Something that he loved
6. The person he wrote a book about
7. Something that he started to become in 1905
8. Something that he and his wife set up for sick people
9. The place where he and his wife worked as missionaries
10. This is what he believed the world needs most (3 words)
11. The number of years that he cared for the sick in the African jungle

TO PRAY AND REMEMBER

PRAYER FOR ANIMALS AND THEIR MASTERS

Hear our humble prayer,
O God,

for our friends, the animals,
especially for animals who are suffering:
for animals that are over-worked,
under-fed, and cruelly treated;
for all wistful creatures in captivity
that beat their wings against bars;
for any that are hunted or lost or deserted
or frightened or hungry;
for all that must be put to death.

We entreat for them all
your mercy and pity,
and for those who deal with them
we ask a heart of compassion
and gentle hands and kindly words.
Make us, ourselves,
to be true friends to animals
and so to share the blessings of the Merciful.
    Albert Schweitzer 1875-1965

(NEW SAINT JOSEPH PEOPLE'S PRAYER BOOK, #598, (p. 480-481)

TO THINK AND TALK ABOUT

1. What prayer did Albert Schweitzer make up as a child that he prayed all his life?
2. In what ways was Albert talented and how did he use his gifts?
3. What was Albert Schweitzer's deepest conviction and how do you feel about it?

TO READ AND ENJOY:

A Storybook:

A THOUSAND PAILS OF WATER by Ronald Roy (Albert A. Knopf, Inc., 201 E. 50 St., New York, N.Y. 10022, 1978)

A Poem:

ALBERT SCHWEITZER

Albert Schweitzer
In the jungle
Eased people's hurt
And people's pain.
He treated life
With reverence
And for this
His life's
Acclaimed.

DATE DUE